FAIRACRES PUBLICATIONS 235

CREATE IN ME A CLEAN HEART

James Coutts

© 2025 SLG Press
First Edition 2025

Fairacres Publications No. 235

Print ISBN 978-0-7283-0314-0
ISSN 0307-1405

SLG Press asserts on behalf of James Coutts his right to be identified as the author of this work in accordance with the Copyright, Designs and Patents Act 1988.

All rights reserved. No part of this publication may be reproduced, stored in a retrieval system, or transmitted, in any form or by any means, electronic, mechanical, photocopying, recording or otherwise, without the prior permission of the copyright owner.

Edited by Tony Dickinson
Typeset in Palatino Linotype by Julia Craig-McFeely

SLG Press
Convent of the Incarnation
Fairacres Oxford
www.slgpress.co.uk

Printed by
Grosvenor Group Ltd, Loughton, Essex

CONTENTS

Exordium	iii
I — The Saviour	1
II — The Holy Spirit	11
III — The Father	20
IV — God the Holy Trinity	30
V — Worship	40
VI — Eucharist	48

EXORDIUM

This series of heartfelt, thought-provoking meditations originated as daily talks focussing a week-long retreat in preparation for Lent given for the Sisters of the Love of God at Fairacres Convent in 1982. However, Lent is not the only time when we might need to stop and make a space to examine our faith and the ways in which it impacts our daily lives and our commitment to God. The intensity of Fr Coutts's words focus us on God and his Son, on his mercy and redeeming love for us, no matter how unworthy we think we are. Indeed our very unworthiness is a matter for rejoicing, since the most unworthy are also the most blessed. These meditations help us to consider and respond to some fundamental questions at any time in our lives:

What is Jesus for me?

What is the meaning of the Cross for me?

Who is the heavenly Father?

What is my relationship with him?

What place does the Eucharist have in my life?

Sometimes we need a little time to stop and reflect about our Christian lives; create for ourselves a time for meaningful reflection and spiritual growth; a time to create a clean heart and start afresh.

CREATE IN ME

A CLEAN HEART

I
THE SAVIOUR

Every day St Antony began again his conversion to God:
'Create in me a clean heart, O Lord; Renew a right spirit within me.'
(Ps. 51:10)[1]

He came down with them and stood on a level place, with a great crowd of his disciples and a great multitude of people from all Judea, Jerusalem, and the coast of Tyre and Sidon. They had come to hear him and to be healed of their diseases; and those who were troubled with unclean spirits were cured. And all in the crowd were trying to touch him, for power came out from him and healed all of them. Then he looked up at his disciples and said: 'Blessed are you who are poor, for yours is the kingdom of God.' (Luke 6:17–20)

WHEN JESUS HAD sat down and saw the great crowd of people gathered around him, he began to read what he saw in the multitude of eyes that were looking at him. What was written in those eyes? A mixture of hope and fear, of anxiety and of secret longing. To begin with, this was the army of the troubled, the guilt-burdened, the lonely, the incurably ill, the outcast. And they gazed at Jesus with the patient, inscrutable eyes that can be fathomed only by the Saviour himself. Few of us have ever seen such an army of the miserable in person, though increasingly they are visible on our television screens in frightful proliferation, not only in distant desert lands, but on our very doorsteps. In our civilization the lonely and those with mental illness that prevents them from being able to function in society are secluded and kept away from us in institutions. But in our Lord's Palestine, there were no such places. Could we bear to look at such a crowd of

---

[1] Paraphrased from Athanasius, *Life of St Anthony*, 7.

crippled, mutilated and desperate people? People without hope, without loving care?

All these people gathered around Jesus for, in some mysterious way, he attracts these poor people to himself. Like a magnet, Jesus draws to himself sinners and sufferers out of their hiding places. In Jesus they recognize something that they do not find in any other person. They see that Jesus stands among them as one of them. Jesus does not behave as if he were one of the great and powerful in the world who build for themselves exclusive residences from which they cannot see the world's misery; who organize coffee-mornings for the poor, but do not open their lives to them.

> Lord, when was it that we saw you? (Matt. 25:37)

Jesus stands among the poor, as a poor man himself. Jesus stands utterly vulnerable and exposed to the pain of the world. He stands therefore within the pain of the world. Paul says:

> For you know the generous act of our Lord Jesus Christ, that though he was rich, yet for your sakes he became poor, so that by his poverty you might become rich. (2 Cor. 8:9)

So these people are grateful to this man who comes among them, who closes neither his eyes, nor his heart to them. But they also recognize something else in Jesus, something far more incomprehensible: they notice that the destructive powers of guilt, anxiety and suffering in the midst of which Jesus stands do not touch his inner being but withdraw before him. Jesus visibly shudders under the attacks of pain and hell, but evil does not enter and possess Jesus's heart as their hearts are possessed. Evil withdraws, powerless and defeated before him. Because of this all these people seek to get near to Jesus. They gaze with wistful longing at his hands that can do so much good, which never tire of healing and blessing. But now these hands are at rest. Now Jesus is sitting down, and he begins to speak.

Do the people feel disappointed? Would they have preferred some practical help: for Jesus to satisfy their hunger, to bind up their wounds, to drive their anxious, mad thoughts from their minds?

Why does he *speak* to them when their misery cries out for action? Theories cannot feed and heal people, cannot fill loneliness, cannot restore to life a dead child. Perhaps they think they know what Jesus is going to say to them. They imagine that

> *He is going speak like John the Baptist.*
>
> *He is going to tell them that their misery and suffering represent a judgement upon them.*
>
> *He is going to urge them to change their behaviour, like John when he told the crowds: 'Even now the axe is lying at the root of the trees, repent.' (Matt. 3:10)*
>
> *He is going to say: it is your fault you are the way you are. Get a grip on yourselves.*

Do they wait for God's anger to be emptied out upon them, these people gathered around him?

> *People weighed down with inner and outer burdens, with suffering,*
>
> *people with terror in their hearts and anxiety in their minds,*
>
> *people carrying meaninglessness and guilt and loneliness.*

To all of them Jesus says, with immeasurable tenderness, *Blessed are you, O how happy you are.*[2]

> Now when Jesus had finished saying these things, the crowds were astounded at his teaching.   (Matt. 7:28)

That is what always happens when God unveils his unexpected goodness, his great tenderness. It is so immense, so utterly beyond what we can give or expect, that we are bewildered by it. It is the awareness of the sheer goodness of God that leads us to repent; it is the sight of the outstretched arms of the Father that breaks the prodigal's heart. Jesus preaches the Beatitudes specifically to those who are in trouble:

---

[2] Cf. Matt. 5:3–12.

To the poor,
to those who suffer because of their shortcomings and failures,
to the persecuted,
to the grieving,
to the sick,
to the hungry,
to the thirsty.

Jesus tells them that they are blessed, happy, blissful. Was that cruel of him? The Beatitudes raise awkward questions for us:

How can you call someone who has cancer blessed?

How can you tell a woman whose marriage has broken down that she is blessed?

How can you tell a person who lives in desperate loneliness that they are blessed?

How can you tell someone who has lost home and country and crossed a continent in search of refuge from war that he is blessed?

We must remember who it is who speaks these words. The Beatitudes are not general maxims, applicable to all and sundry. Jesus himself spoke to each member of this crowd, and he speaks now to each of us. To our generation he says:

Everywhere in the world there is sin and guilt, suffering and death, but I, the Crucified One, roll these powers back.

The first reason why you who are miserable are to be called blessed, is simply that I am in the midst of you as your Saviour.

You complain that you are full of anxiety, that you have to suffer? Look, I myself, the Son of God, creation's Alpha and Omega, found my real self and learned obedience in what I suffered.

You complain that you have to drink a bitter cup? Look what I myself drank, as I prayed in the garden of Gethsemane: 'Father, take this cup away from me'. There I discovered peace and accepted the Father's will.

You complain that in your sufferings you cannot see the face of God nor feel his presence. I too had the same experience of godforsakenness. I, too, screamed out, 'My God, my God, why hast thou forsaken me?' and while my tortured body drooped, but could not fall because I was pinioned by nails, suddenly there was the Father's hand upholding me, all around me waiting to receive me.

You are blessed and happy because I who have shared your suffering. I, who have tasted and come through your death, I am in the midst of you, as your brother and Saviour.

So, come to me, you who labour and are heavy laden, and I will give you rest. Take my yoke upon you, for it is lighter than the yoke anyone else wants to put on you.

Whatever has been our experience of life, by whatever spiritual path we have travelled to reach this place, it is *we* who are the poor, so it is us whom Jesus calls blessed. Not because of what we are, still less because of our Christian experience: but we are blessed and blissful in this: that Jesus himself is in our midst as our Saviour. Jesus the Word of God, the beloved of the Father, sender of the Spirit, stands among us. He has called us to come to him.

> You did not choose me but I chose you. And I appointed you to go and bear fruit. (John 15:16)

That is the blessedness, the sole purpose of these meditations: to be in the presence of the Saviour. To learn afresh what it is to know Jesus and to be known by him; what it is to love Jesus and to be loved by him. And if we know that we do not love and do not know and cannot even long for him with our whole heart, then we are indeed the poor and we must leap and be glad, for seeing our need he can come to us. That is the Gospel, the Good News; Jesus Christ has seen me and loves me. There is no place where his love does not reach; there is no individual his arms do not encompass:

The security a babe has in its mother's arms;

the fragility of a nutshell floating on a stream towards the ocean;

What is Poverty?

> *Complete poverty, absolute nothingness ... before absolute Allness;*
>
> *poverty of understanding, of knowledge ...*

The Psalmist writes:

> I was stupid and ignorant; I was like a brute beast toward you. Nevertheless I am continually with you; you hold my right hand.
>
> (Ps. 73:23)

Those words remind us that I am simply a 'brute beast', a blind lump, heaving itself up to God by its desires: blessed are the poor, blessed are the lumps, those who long to know their need, to be re-centred on the Saviour.

The Kingdom is already beginning to be theirs. The Lord is their future, and is becoming their present. Jesus is God the Father's poverty, in front of us. Jesus is the Father's searching love, in front of us. And our searching love, in front of the Father. Jesus put mankind's question to God and God's question to mankind. Mankind's question to God is always: 'My God, my God, why hast thou forsaken me?' (Matt. 27:46), even though it may come to us in other words:

> *What is the meaning of this disease in my body?*
>
> *Why do you allow my body to suffer?*
>
> *Is there any point to the mass graves of Katyn, Auschwitz, or El Salvador?*
>
> *Is there any purpose in my life?*

God's question to us is: 'Who do you say that I am?' (Matt. 16:13), and everyone in history who hears the Gospel has heard that question in some form, and has striven to answer it.

The twelve disciples tried unsuccessfully to contain Jesus within definitions and categories: their minds jumped over more and more fences, as they tried to pin Jesus down. He was a teacher, with extraordinary

> Who am I, Jesus, for you?

authority who took the ancient scriptural authority of the Old Testament and nurtured it into something more.

> You have heard that it was said by Moses ... but I say unto you ...
> (Matt. 5:38)

Jesus's teaching enlarged their understanding of God, of other people, and of themselves, but he also healed physical, mental and spiritual disorders. Consider for a moment what it must have been like to be the demoniac whose name was Legion? Hitherto the man had always managed to terrify people with his clashing chains and strange behaviour, but now he finds himself before the face of Jesus, with Jesus looking calmly and with healing power into his eyes.

To the disciples therefore Jesus is more than a prophet: he is a healer of the body and the spirit and he exemplified a perfection that had never been seen before. People tried to catch him out or trip him up in his teachings, but they failed; they said that he never sinned, an absolutely extraordinary thing. He was completely human, (the Son of Man) and also completely from the Other (Son of God). He demanded that The Twelve left everything to become his disciples. What, then, did they make of his death on the Cross?

Afterwards, for them, everything was new and enlarged: he was with them again, their lives were turned upside down and inside out, transformed, transfigured, triumphant, and full of joy. As Gerard Manley Hopkins wrote:

> ... Flesh fade, and mortal trash
> Fall to the residuary worm; world's wildfire, leave but ash:
>   In a flash, at a trumpet crash,
> I am all at once what Christ is, since he was what I am, and
> This Jack, joke, poor potsherd, patch, matchwood, immortal diamond,
>   Is immortal diamond.[3]

---

[3] Gerard Manley Hopkins, 'That Nature is a Heraclitean Fire and of the Comfort of the Resurrection'.

Who is this Man-in-Jesus and what therefore are those who are now with him? For he sets a question mark against their old lives. They have to become like him:

Poor in spirit
meek
mourning
hungering and thirsting for righteousness
merciful
pure in heart
peace-creators
persecuted for righteousness' sake.

In those words are the eight questions that the Lord sets against our life-style and our motives. How do I measure up to them? I know that if I am a very long way from fulfilling them, still, Jesus comes to me out of the Beatitudes as the one who does fulfil them, as the one whom they describe. And so he can heal us. Confronted by the Lord, either I can react with

self-assertion,
violence,
faithlessness,
doing what is right in my own eyes.

Or I can react with the attitude of Mary, with

faith,
docility to the word,
poverty,
transparency to God.

In Dostoevsky's *Crime and Punishment*, Sonia has been driven to becoming a prostitute because of the needs of her family. Her friend, the student Raskolnikov, thinks that there are three possibilities ahead of her: suicide, the mad house, or to sink into 'depravity which obscures the mind and turns the heart to stone'.[4] Sonia reads to

---

[4] Fyodor Dostoyevsky, *Crime and Punishment*, trans. Constance Garnett, Wordsworth Classics (Wordsworth Editions, 2000), 175–6.

Raskolnikov the story of the resurrection of Lazarus. She explains to him what it is to have to die, and to be judged. But also what it is to know him who alone can make all things new. Squeezing his hand, she whispers, 'What should I be without God?'

Her answer is that without God there would be only guilt and punishment, darkness, disease, the death of her heart, the death of her body. But she lives in hope of a miracle, the miracle of forgiveness and resurrection. Lazarus gives her the hope of redemption.

What should we be without the God who raised up Lazarus? The God who, in that wonderful miracle, breaks through the inevitability of disease and punishment and death? The God who judges, and in so doing makes all things new. Only in the place of death can there be the miracle of resurrection. Repentance is to live in the hope of a miracle: the miracle of seeing the Father running out of heaven as Jesus Christ on the Cross, waving and beckoning, putting a ring on my finger and the best robe upon me. 'What is man without God? What would I be without the Lord?' Happy are those who are poor, for the Saviour is standing among them. Holy Saviour, Blessed are the poor in all their struggles as Charles Wesley recognized: the Kingdom is already beginning to be theirs.

> Come, O Thou Traveller unknown,
> Whom still I hold, but cannot see!
> My Company before is gone,
> And I am left alone with Thee;
> With Thee all night I mean to stay,
> And wrestle till the break of day.
>
> I need not tell Thee who I am,
> My misery and sin declare;
> Thyself hast called me by my name;
> Look on Thy hands, and read it there:
> But who, I ask Thee, who art thou?
> Tell me Thy name, and tell me now.

In vain Thou strugglest to get free;
I never will unloose my hold!
Art Thou the Man that died for me?
The secret of Thy love unfold:
Wrestling, I will not let Thee go,
Till I Thy name, thy nature know.

Yield to me now; for I am weak,
But confident in self-despair;
Speak to my heart, in blessings speak,
Be conquered by my instant prayer;
Speak, or Thou never hence shalt move,
And tell me if Thy name is Love.

'Tis Love! 'tis Love! Thou diedst for me!
I hear Thy whisper in my heart;
The morning breaks, the shadows flee,
Pure, universal Love Thou art;
To me, to all, Thy mercies move:
Thy nature and Thy name is Love.

Charles Wesley[5]

> *Father, we thank you, for by our baptism you have made us yours.*

---

[5] *The Methodist Hymn and Tune Book* (The Methodist Book and Publishing House, 1917), no. 445.

II
THE HOLY SPIRIT

Father, by thy Holy Spirit, lead me in paths of righteousness.

IN THE BIBLE, God speaks and communicates with us through his Word, so God knows himself through his Spirit.

> For what human being knows what is truly human except the human spirit that is within? So also no one comprehends what is truly God's except the Spirit of God. (1 Cor. 2:11)

Paul is saying that like can only be known by like; therefore mankind cannot know God since no finite spirit can understand infinite spirit: moreover (a bigger problem) we have severed ourselves from God, and gone our own way and are busy destroying our neighbours and the creation by sin. God's Spirit is God's self-knowledge. When God gives his spirit, he is thereby giving a share in his own self-understanding, his own knowledge of himself as Trinity.

Jesus during his earthly life was (as he still remains) the perfect receiver of the Spirit: quite simply, he is 'led by the Spirit' and the Spirit descends upon him. All four gospels tell us that after his baptism in Jordan, there was a new outpouring of the Holy Spirit. We cannot enter into Jesus's self-understanding, but we must affirm that in his life he grew and developed in wisdom, in the understanding of his own identity and mission and in his experience of the power of the Spirit to fulfil that mission. After his baptism, he is driven by the Spirit into the desert and on his return he proclaims,

> The Spirit of the Lord is upon me, because he has appointed me to preach good news to the poor. He has sent me to proclaim release to captives, and recovering of sight to the blind, to set at liberty those who are oppressed, to proclaim the acceptable year of the Lord. (Luke 4:18–29)

Jesus promised that when he was glorified, he would give to his followers the very same Spirit which he had himself received from the Father. The mystery of Pentecost, the outpouring of the Spirit, the third Person of the Holy Trinity, is not simply for the first generation of disciples but it is for the life of every disciple.

> I will pour out my spirit upon all flesh ... (Acts 2:17)

In his address to the crowd at Pentecost Peter quotes Joel 2:28, and he adds, 'the promise is made to you and to your children, and for all who are far away, for all whom the Lord our God will call to himself' (Acts 2:39). The Father, through the exalted Jesus, sends the Holy Spirit upon Jesus's community. Through the Spirit, the exalted Jesus manifests his presence and his lordship over the creation. Thus the gift of the Spirit is the dawn of a new eon. The purpose of the gift of the Spirit is to point us to the Cross of Jesus as the act and place of Salvation: thereby the Spirit sets the believer in the sphere of the power of the Crucified. Through the Spirit, the exalted Lord seizes control in our hearts; and conversely by his Spirit we are led to and incorporated into the exalted Lord. The Spirit takes us into the Kingdom.

BAPTISM

It is, of course, baptism that imparts the Spirit to every believer; thus it is baptism that assures us of our share in Jesus's kingdom of the resurrection. By the gift of the Spirit, therefore, the unbridgeable gulf between the spirit of humans and the Spirit of God is overcome. As St Paul tells the Christians of Rome,

> you have received a spirit of adoption. When we cry 'Abba: Father!' it is that very Spirit bearing witness with our spirit that we are children of God.   (Rom. 8:15–16)

What very gloomy expectations we have of God! When we return in repentance to our dear Father, we get ready to say to him, 'Make me one of your hired servants.' We even want our repentance to be on our own self-hating terms! 'Never can I expect to share your living room and family circle, Lord, give me a little lean-to behind the cowshed. I'll do every duty you prescribe. I won't be a nuisance to you—treat me as one of your servants.'

But the dear Father will not have us back on those gloomy terms, as servants; he wants us back as the dear children of his love, as sharers of his glory. The Spirit does not establish an *intellectual* knowledge *about* God but a new wondering relationship *with* the Father, and therefore with his Son. This new relationship is summed up in two joyful exclamations: 'Abba! Father' and 'Jesus is Lord!' (Rom. 8:15–16; Gal. 4:6). God calls us to share in his own Trinitarian relationship and communion of love. The Spirit is the Spirit of Truth, maintaining the disciples in the teaching of Jesus, guiding them to Jesus who is Truth. Thus this work of the Spirit glorifies Jesus, for just as Jesus glorified the Father in his mission on the soil of Palestine, so the Spirit glorifies Jesus in the soil of the lives of the disciples. Jesus will be theirs, they will belong to him, they are included in the mighty and transforming benefits of his death and resurrection. Jesus's life and work will be reflected and extended in them: such is the work of the Spirit.

The Spirit is given in baptism. Ignatius of Antioch says, 'There is within me a living stream which cries "Come to the Father".'[6]

Another story from the desert tells of the three brothers who want to serve God: The first decides to become a doctor and a healer, the second decides to become a lawyer and to make reconciliation between people. The third goes off into the desert. After a few years, the doctor is overcome with despair, and goes to see the lawyer who is disillusioned by people's acquisitiveness and aggression. Together they go to visit the hermit, to whom they explain their feelings. He fills a bucket of water from the stream. At first the three men cannot see anything in the bucket, because the water is disturbed with silt. After a while the silt settles down and they are

---

[6] St Ignatius, *Epistle to the Romans*, Ch. 7, 'Reason of desiring to die'.

able to see their own reflections in the water.[7] For me this resonates with the words of Jesus:

> 'Let anyone who is thirsty come to me, and let the one who believes in me drink. As the scripture has said, "Out of the believer's heart shall flow rivers of living water".' Now he said this about the Spirit ... for as yet there was no Spirit, because Jesus was not yet glorified. (John 7:37–9)

The water bubbles and rises within us to everlasting life. It is the same stream that proceeds from the Father and the Son.

It is as if part of our response to Christ is to hold our heart still before the Father, so that the heart and its confusion, ignorance, and selfishness in which we live, and which we are, can be still, and we can begin to see our true reflection in this water; so that we can begin to see the new and glorious person that God is calling us to become. Perhaps it is as if our heart is like a bucket of water and our ascetic effort is to hold our heart still before the face of the Father, for us to be reflections of the Father's image. In this symbol, the water in my heart is both my spirit and the Holy Spirit; when my heart is still before God, then I can begin to discern the relationship between myself and the Holy Spirit. Then truly takes place the second creation when the Holy Spirit of God moves upon the dark places and the void of sin, as we echo the words of the Psalmist,

Make in me a clean heart.

> Create in me a clean heart, O God,
> and put a new and right spirit within me.
> Do not cast me away from your presence,
> and do not take your holy spirit from me. (Ps. 51:10–11)

My heart is full of distraction, confusion, mixed motives, sinfulness. My heart is not yet enlightened, not yet what God wants it to be. I need a new spirit within me. St John Chrysostom says, 'find

---

[7] Benedicta Ward SLG, *The Wisdom of the Desert Fathers: Systematic Sayings from the Anonymous Series of the* Apophthegmata Patrum, Fairacres Publications 48 (Oxford: SLG Press, 1986), 1 (saying no. 2).

the door to your heart, and you will find the door to the kingdom', implying that we are on the outside.[8] We just need to find the door to our true self. There is a strange interaction between seeking and being still; between striving and listening.

Those words of Jesus, 'the kingdom of heaven has suffered violence, and the violent take it by force' (Matt. 11:12) suggest that we must seek with great perseverance and determination. Our desire to enter the kingdom must be violent! At the same time, 'Hold thee still in the Lord and abide patiently upon him' (Ps. 37:1). One of the Desert Fathers says: 'The heart is like a pond. Dig deeper into the pond and the water gets clearer and clearer. Toss in dung and it gets fouled up.'

Silence, waiting, holding oneself still and empty, is a way of scooping out that void in us. It is a way of burrowing down to increase the draught that God will give, as he promises the prophet:

> I will pour water upon the thirsty land　　　　(Is. 44:3)

New space must be made available in our heart for God, where we can pierce through to the source of our being. That source is the Spirit within us: we are born of that water and Spirit. New life rises in our hearts like a spring of clear water: and all at once it fills to the brim the space which silence has made available in us. So we hear the words of the Psalmist,

> Be still before the Lord, and wait patiently for him.　(Ps. 37:7)

and we return to the insight of St Ignatius:

> There is within me a living stream which cries 'Come to the Father'.

In addition to the image of the spring of water, there is the image of the sentry. Paul urges his disciples to watch and pray. Stand on your toes, be alert. I remember when I was a child being fascinated by an old book about the Boer War, *With the Flag to Pretoria*. In my copy the frontispiece depicted a

> Watch and Pray.

---

[8] Quoted in Hannah Ward and Jennifer Wild, *The Westminster Collection of Christian Meditations* (John Knox Press, 2000), 98.

sentry standing on the perimeter of the camp at night. He is totally alert, with loaded rifle in his hand and is staring out into the bush that surrounds the camp. his task is to distinguish between the various sounds that come to him from the undergrowth. Is it just some animal moving in the bush, or is it a secret enemy crawling up to attack? So the disciple, too, is on sentry duty on the perimeter of his own heart, and on the perimeter of creation. He has to distinguish between the various sense-impressions that come to his heart. His task is, in St John's words, to 'test the spirits to see whether they are from God' (1 John 4:1).

Do not allow every impression, every spirit, into your heart. In his prayer, the disciple stands watching, on guard at the door of his heart, turning aside memories, distractions, and daydreams—'bringing every thought into captivity to the law of Christ' (2 Cor. 10:5), only allowing the exalted Jesus entry into his heart. The disciple also stands at the perimeter of the world, because he is keeping his heart empty for the Lord, for the sake of the world, so that the water may flow through him to the parched world.

The sentry's task is not simply the negative one of turning aside each distraction; it is also the positive one of allowing entry only to the exalted Lord. The watchful disciple wants to stand in front of Jesus, to meet Jesus face-to-face, so that he can love him. This means that the watchful disciple has passed far beyond the stage of being the prodigal son who wishes to enter again into a new and forgiven relationship with the Lord. Nor does the watchful disciple cherish in his memory any unrepented sin because if that is happening then this memory of the past, this sinful ambition in the present, will come and stand between him and the exalted Lord. No, the supreme and only desire of the disciple is to stand in front of the Lord and to meet him in joy and reconciliation and triumph.

The watchful disciple stands before the Lord in peace. He remembers the Lord's word:

> when you are offering your gift at the altar, if you remember that your brother or sister has something against you, leave your gift

there before the altar and go; first be reconciled to your brother
or sister, and then come and offer your gift.   (Matt. 5:23–4)

Before we can be alert and watchful before the face of God, we must first be at peace with our brother, not only our physical interactions but also our internal strife. I believe the Greek word *eirene* (peace) comes from the word *eiro*, meaning 'I bind together, I unite'.

There are three 'brothers' with whom the watchful disciple must first be united and at peace. He must be at peace with the Lord Jesus, he must be reconciled to him and have his sins forgiven. Then again, he must be at peace with his own heart, with his own body and conscience. We must have accepted ourselves, this particular body, this background, these relationships under which I have failed, this disease in my body, this particular death in front of me. I must have repented of my sin and accepted the thought that God has forgiven me. I must be at peace with myself, with all the nerve-endings of my body. My heart must not be distracted. It must be united in peace. And thirdly, the disciple must be at peace with the things he handles: with his garden, the kitchen, and the car. All these areas of his life must be worthy of God.

Here is a very simple picture from the ritual book of the Sioux. Black Elk is talking about the peace pipe and he says the mouthpiece is of animal horn, the stem is wood, the bowl of the pipe is made of stone, and eagle feathers are hanging down from it. He says,

> The peace pipe is sacred because when you are smoking the pipe, you are at one with the stone, with the birds, with the animals, with the elk. When you are smoking the pipe, you are reconciled to creation.[9]

So before the watchful disciple can come and stand before the Lord, he must have made a mini-reconciliation with himself, with all

---

[9] Paraphrased from Joseph Epes Brown, *The Sacred Pipe: Black Elk's Account of the Seven Rites of the Oglala Sioux*, The Civilization of the American Indian Series 36 (Penguin 1973; repr. University of Oklahoma Press, 2012), 3.

these dimensions of his relationships. So now he comes and stands alert and watchful and in peace before the face of God. He turns away everything that is not God; he comes to Jesus waiting in front of him, face to face, with a heart full of concentration, waiting, watching, loving, in adoration. Stand therefore. The objectivity of that relationship: God is, and I stand in front of him.

> The Lord of hosts lives, before whom I stand. (1 Kings 18:15)

Remember all the stories of the desert about watchfulness. About people who simply stood and waited in front of God. There is Abba Lot's query of Abba Joseph of Panephysis, 'Will I be able to persevere in prayer?' And the old man holds up his hand against the setting sun so that the enquirer can't look at it any more. And he replies, 'If you desire it, you shall be wholly aflame.'[10]

That is the challenge to us: *If you desire it ...* Does my response echo that of Julian of Norwich, when she prayed:

> God of your goodness give me yourself,
> for if I ask anything that is less than thee,
> ever shall I be wanting;
> only in thee have I all.

Julian of Norwich tells us that 'the continual seeking of the soul pleaseth God full greatly: for it may do no more than seek, suffer, and trust.'[11]

All this standing, and waiting, and longing; all this making God our centre and our future, is part of the grace of the Holy Spirit in our lives: the Spirit who brings us into a relationship with the Father, crying 'Abba!' in our hearts; the Spirit who sets us completely under the triumphant Lordship of Jesus the Victor. The growth of our experience of the Spirit is not limited to the growth in this life, but our

---

[10] https://www.johnsanidopoulos.com/2017/06/life-and-sayings-of-holy-abba-joseph.html (accessed 26 February 2021).

[11] Julian of Norwich, *Revelations of Divine Love*, ed. Roger Hudleston (Dover, 2012), 66–7.

deepening, wondering relationship with God will be deepened by grace throughout all eternity. As St Paul recognized,

> all of us, with unveiled faces, seeing the glory of the Lord as though reflected in a mirror, are being transformed into the same image from one degree of glory to another; for this comes from the Lord, the Spirit. (2 Cor. 3:18)

> Father of Jesus, we thank you that even now we 'are being changed into his likeness from one degree of glory to another' (2 Cor. 3:18).

III
THE FATHER

Lord, show us the Father, and we will be satisfied. (John 14:8)

THE VERY HEART of the Gospel is the hidden and constant relationship of Jesus with his Father. This relationship is for him, the still point in the turning world. The secret of the gospel is Jesus's relationship, his turning towards the Father. Throughout the earthly ministry, Jesus comes to people from the Father: the knowledge of this relationship provides the security and source of Jesus's life. Moreover Jesus constantly renews his relationship with the Father, rising early in the morning to pray to him. Thus it is the Father's salvation and word that Jesus brings to the people.

> In the beginning was the Word, and the Word was with God.
> (John 1:1)

The word 'with' is translated from the Greek *pros* which means literally 'towards'. The Word is towards God: the eternal orientation and conversion of the Son towards his Father. The person of Jesus is the living word spoken eternally by the Father. In a certain anthropomorphic way we might say that the word 'Jesus', is the only human word which the Father eternally utters: the Father eternally begets his Word. He gives himself eternally in the begetting of the Word: Jesus is the 'brightness of the Father's glory, the express image of his person.' (Heb. 1:3) The Son, the Word, is the visibility of the invisible, as light comes from light, so he is God from God.

For us the meaning of the word 'Father' is not discovered by looking at any human relationship, but simply by considering the relationship between *Jesus* and his Father. God's fatherhood is not human fatherhood projected on to some heavenly background, nor is God's fatherhood in any way comparable to pagan ideas of God as father. In pagan myths, God's fatherhood implies a physical and sexual marriage between the gods and the human women, or, as in Baal religion, the earth mother has to be fertilized year by year by the sky-father in a ritual of sacred procreation, in order that the land might become married and fertile. So the Old Testament is reticent about speaking of God as Father, for fear of being misinterpreted in this pagan way, and implying that God has a physical, generative, relationship with his people.

The Old Testament sense of the transcendent distance between the Creator and his creation, between the holy Judge and sinful, rebellious mankind, made it hesitate to use any concept of the Father that could imply any human or physical relationship between God and people. On the rare occasions in the Old Testament where God is described as the Father of Israel, it is in terms of the historical election of the people. They are God's adopted sons, it is therefore part of God's covenant responsibility to protect and care for them: their part is to honour, trust and obey God, The emphasis is not on similarity of nature between God and the people, but on God's absolute and free choice: not on generation, but election: not on physical relationship but on a covenant relationship of grace on the one part and of obedience on the other. Psalm 103 is prepared to compare the Lord's compassion to that of a father, but not actually to say that God is father.

> As a father has compassion for his children, so the Lord has compassion for those who fear him. (Ps. 103:13)

All four gospels agree that Jesus addressed God as 'Abba' and that he used this address in all his prayers except one, the cry of dereliction on the Cross, where he appears to be quoting Psalm 22. As we have seen, nowhere in the Old Testament do we find God addressed as 'father'. The word 'Abba' is the word small and grown-up children use to their father. Jeremias says: 'Jesus spoke to God as a child to his father: confidently and securely and yet at the same time reverently and obediently.'[12] The maintenance of the Aramaic word in the life of the New Testament church indicates how special the church knew the word to be for Jesus and how special the word was for them.

The word 'Abba' is *first* recorded in the Gospels in the garden of Gethsemane and it is from that experience that we can tease out the meaning of the Fatherhood of God:

> And going a little farther, he threw himself on the ground and prayed, 'My Father [Abba], if it is possible, let this cup pass from me; yet not what I want but what you want.' (Matt. 26:39)

To be the Son of this Father, to address and relate to him as 'Abba' implies Jesus conforming his will to the Father's and this to the extreme extent of drinking the cup of immeasurable suffering. The obedience of the unique Son is a unique obedience greater than that required of any other. As Philippians 2:8 puts it, 'obedient unto death, even death on a cross'.

The Father who makes this demand is no stern lawgiver threatening punishment, promulgating irrational, arbitrary demands. The Father Jesus addressed as 'Abba' in Gethsemane is the Father whom he has proved to be, reliable in his promises and utterly faithful in his love. Jesus obeys the Father's will that calls him to the Cross, with hope and expectation, because it is the will of the Father whose love he has experienced and can trust. He goes to the Cross, not driven by some blind demand, but in response to trusting and expectant love. Here we begin to understand that the Father's love

> *Evokes*
>> *Stretches*
>>> *Begets*
>>>> *Creates.*

The Son's love

> *Responds*
>> *Obeys.*

---

[12] Joachim Jeremias, *New Testament Theology* (SCM Press, 1971), 67.

In Gethsemane and on the Cross, Jesus the new creation, responds with a loving and complete *Yes* to the Father, making a response that the old creation did not make. But it is important to remember that the initiator in this work of salvation and re-creation is the Father's searching love. There is no question of the Son making atonement to the Father or trying to get the Father to change his mind, or of the Father requiring satisfaction or imposing punishment. It is the Father himself who suffers as he gives the sacrifice; who does what Abraham did not have to do, in the sacrifice of his son Isaac. Paul constantly stresses the Father as the source of atoning love, as when he writes,

> All this is from God, who reconciled us to himself through Christ, ... in Christ God was reconciling the world to himself
> (2 Cor. 5:18–19)

> But God proves his love for us in that while we still were sinners Christ died for us. (Rom. 5:8)

St John includes a similar thought in the conversation between Jesus and Nicodemus: 'For God so loved the world that he gave his only Son.' (John 3:16).

ATONEMENT

The love of God is not the result of atonement but its precondition: God is the *origin* of atonement. God is also the *agent* of atonement, for only God can deal with the universal and cosmic dimensions of salvation, which must include everyone, all creation. And also, God is the *object* of atonement. The purpose of atonement is not just the conversion of the ungodly, but it is the removal of the divine judgement that stands against the sinner—a judgement that can only be removed by being taken away by the Lamb given by God himself.

On the Cross the Son is dealing with his Father, rather than with us. On our behalf, he is offering the active obedience that fulfils his Father's will: there he offers the trust and obedience that alone can respond to and is worthy of the Father's love: there he suffers the Father's judgement and damnation upon sinners, because only thus can sinful people have their guilt taken away and receive new life. There on the Cross he suffers the abandonment that his Father's judgement decrees for the ungodly. I think it is Fr Stăniloae who said that by the Cross God descended into his own absence so that everything might become God.[13]

We can perhaps best understand the atonement in terms of the parable of the prodigal son. The unfortunate son presumably said to himself, *My father is a just man. He is strict and upright and no one can pull the wool over his eyes. I can't face him when I think of what I have done to him, done to the family, done to myself.* But at the same time he thinks: *Nevertheless, my Father suffers from my misery because I am not with him, for he loves me, he won't give me up. I am his child: he has surely put a light in his window as a sign of his love waiting for me, he is longing for me to come home.*

Both those voices blend in the heart of the prodigal. One says, *My father is righteous and holy, I cannot appear before him in my depraved condition.* The other says, *Nevertheless, he calls me to come.*

The paradox of God's righteous love is that it shows me both that I am wounded, always wounded, and therefore that I need always to come to him to be healed and restored. The righteous love always both wounds and heals. What happens when you forgive another person? It doesn't mean that you can forget the injury. What it means is that you yourself step into the other person's shoes and say, 'The very motives that made you mean, guilty, hateful to me, are in my heart also: we are absolutely two of a kind.' If I say to my neighbour, 'I forgive you', then what I am saying is not, 'What you have done doesn't matter.' Rather I say, 'What you did was very wrong: but I know from looking at myself how confused, fearful and wicked the human heart is. I could do and I do do exactly what you have done. The evil is coiled up in me as well, so

---

[13] See Dumitru Stăniloae, 'Eternity and Time', trans. A. M. Allchin in *Time*, Fairacres Publications 208 (SLG Press, 2023).

I'll suffer through it with you. I really am in your shoes. I share your burden of guilt also.'

When I choose to forgive another person I am deciding to share his guilt and become at his side a burden-bearer. And it is this solidarity that creates the opportunity for something new and unexpected to happen: for forgiveness to take place.

This is precisely what happens on Calvary. In the suffering, crucified Son, the Father himself steps beside us. He himself bears all the temptations, doubts, perils of our heart. He takes upon himself everything human: suffering, anxiety, loneliness, guilt, doubt, fear of death. He himself enters human finitude and forsakenness. When he screams out, 'My God, my God, why have you forsaken me?' it is because the Son suffers all that we suffer in our separation from God. Nothing can separate God from me because he has become my brother, even in my death. At the bottom of every abyss, he stands beside me. God—or rather Jesus Christ—stands at the very point where judgement must fall upon us. The human intellect can only stammer this truth, but truth it is, through which we become transformed and renewed. I am no longer identified with my past. As Paul writes to the Galatians, 'it is no longer I who live, but it is Christ who lives in me' (Gal. 2:20).

There is a miracle of transformation. I am the companion and brother of my Saviour: nothing can separate me from him. Now when anguish grasps for me, Jesus takes my place with his anguish. There he is with his death, when my death comes looking for me. This insight is well expressed by John Bunyan when he writes:

> So I saw that as Christian came up to the Cross his burden loosed from off his shoulders and began to tumble and so continued to do till it came to the mouth of Christ's sepulchre where it fell in and then I saw it no more. Then was Christian glad and lightsome, and he said with a merry heart, 'Christ hath given me rest by his sorrow, and life by his death.'[14]

---

[14] John Bunyan, *Pilgrim's Progress*, in *The Select Works of John Bunyan* (W. Collins, Sons and Company, 1869), 28.

And by Martin Luther in his exposition of the Letter to the Galatians:o

> Faith therefore must be purely taught: namely that thou art so entirely and nearly joined unto Christ, that he and thou art made as it were one person; so that thou mayest boldly say, I am now one with Christ, that is to say, Christ's righteousness, victory and life are mine. And again, Christ may say, I am that sinner, that is, his sins and his death are mine because he is united and joined unto me, and I unto him.[15]

We are flesh of Christ's flesh, bone of his bone, so that we are nearer to Christ than is a husband to his wife. In the atonement it is not so much vicarious punishment on the Cross but rather the vicarious victory for us. Sinful mankind triumphing in the risen Christ. Jürgen Moltmann has drawn out some of the implications of this for us. He writes that:

> Paul says 'God made him sin for us and he became accursed for us.' Thus in the total, inextricable abandonment of Jesus by his God and Father, Paul sees the delivering up of the Son for godless and godforsaken man. Because God did not spare his Son, all the godless are saved. Though they are godless, they are not god-forsaken, precisely because God has abandoned his own Son and has delivered him up for them. Thus the delivering up of the Son to God-forsakenness is grounds for the justification of the godless. The Father delivers up his Son on the Cross in order to be the Father of those who are delivered up. The Son is delivered up to his death in order to become the Lord of all, both the dead and the living. To understand what happened between Jesus and his God and Father on the Cross, it is necessary to talk in Trinitarian terms. The Son suffers dying, the Father suffers the death of his Son. The grief of the Father is here just as important as the death of the Son. The Fatherlessness of the Son is matched by the Sonlessness of the Father, and if God has constituted himself as the Father of

---

[15] Martin Luther, *A Commentary on Saint Paul's Epistle to the Galatians*, trans. Erasmus Middleton (Robert Carter, 1833), 126.

Jesus then he also suffers the death of his Fatherhood in the death of his Son.[16]

He continues:

> All human history, however much it may be determined by guilt and death, is taken up into the Trinity and integrated in that future history of God. There is no suffering which in this history of God is not God's suffering; no death which has not been God's death in the history of Golgotha. Therefore there is no life, no fortune and no joy which have not been integrated by his history into the eternal life and the eternal joy of God.[17]

So Jesus cries out in Matthew's Gospel:

> I thank you, Father, Lord of heaven and earth, because you have hidden these things from the wise and the intelligent and have revealed them to infants; yes, Father, for such was your gracious will. All things have been handed over to me by my Father; and no one knows the Son except the Father, and no one knows the Father except the Son and anyone to whom the Son chooses to reveal him. 'Come to me, all you that are weary and are carrying heavy burdens, and I will give you rest. Take my yoke upon you, and learn from me; for I am gentle and humble in heart, and you will find rest for your souls. For my yoke is easy, and my burden is light.' (Matt. 11:25–30)

That passage summarizes and emphasizes the concept that the Son is not the primary possessor of what he reveals to his disciples. It has been given to them by the Father. Only the Father knows the Son (the knowledge of his likeness). Similarly, no one knows the Father except in the form of this Son and those to whom this Son chooses to reveal him. This relationship of Son to Father and Father to Son is what the Gospel is about. And on the basis of this relationship and

---

[16] Jürgen Moltmann, *The Crucified God: The Cross of Christ as the Foundation and Criticism of Christian Theology*, trans. R. A. Wilson and J. Bowden (SCM Press, 1974), 242–3.

[17] Moltmann, *The Crucified God*, 246.

longing to include us in that relationship, the Son cries out: 'Come to me all who labour and are heavy laden' (Matt. 11:28). I am the Gospel, I am come to take you to my Father. Salvation is to know Jesus as the Son of Abba, 'Whoever has seen me has seen the Father' (John 14:9). Salvation is to know the Father as the Father of this Son. At the Last Supper Jesus tells the Twelve,

> Those who love me will keep my word, and my Father will love them, and we will come to them and make our home with them.
> (John 14:23)

We note the extraordinary phrase with which Luke introduces Jesus's prayer: 'In that same hour, he rejoiced in the Holy Spirit …' (Luke 10:21–2). In some anthropomorphic sense the Holy Spirit enables the Son to have a relationship with his Father. He is the bond and agent of the relationship between the Father and the Son.

I offer two quotations for contemplation, both written in Wales: The first from Walter Cradock (*c.* 1606–1659), a Puritan Congregationalist minister:

> … one that is fond of God with an holy fondness, he knows he may leap into his fathers lap at any time, and fall into his arms, and ask any thing without courting, and complement.[18]

and the second from Gerard Manley Hopkins

> I say more: the just man justices;
> Keeps grace: that keeps all his goings graces;
> Acts in God's eye what in God's eye he is—
> Christ—for Christ plays in ten thousand places,
> Lovely in limbs, and lovely in eyes not his
> To the Father through the features of men's faces.[19]

---

[18] Walter Cradock, *Divine Drops, Distilled from the Fountain of the Holy Scriptures* (R. W. for Rapha Harford, 1650), 49.

[19] From 'As Kingfishers Catch Fire'.

> The apostle says, 'through Christ we have access in one spirit to the Father.' Lord, Father, we thank you that this is so.

IV
GOD THE HOLY TRINITY

Blessed be the God and Father of our Lord Jesus Christ, who has filled us with all spiritual blessings and chosen us to live to the praise of his glory. (Eph. 1:3)

WHEN WE COME to speak about the Trinity, we need to remember the dictum, *those who speak don't know, and those who know, don't speak*.[20] For, precisely because he is God, he is hidden completely beyond our understanding. *Un dieu complètement defini est un dieu fini* (a god who is completely defined is a finite god).[21] But this inarticulacy, this silence before God, is not the silence of emptiness but of wonder. It is the deep silence: of one who is speechless in awe, speechless before the fullness of him who fills and transcends all things. We are reminded that:

The negative, apophatic approach has to grow out of the positive;

unknowing must be preceded by knowing;

blind prayer must be informed by intellectual discipline of bible reading and rumination.

> In him we live and move and have our being. (Acts 17:28)

To go back to first principles: God is present to us as the ground of our being. God is to us what the image on the television screen is to the actor in the studio. God's presence is in the wing of a butterfly, the petal of the flower, the destructiveness of a tornado.

---

[20] Lao Tze, *Tao te Ch'ing*.

[21] Éliphas Lévi, *Le livre des splendeurs contenant le soleil judaïque, la gloire chrétienne et l'étoile flamboyante* (Chamuel, 1894), 289. The play on words is impossible to render in English.

St Antony the Great, the outstanding representative of the desert tradition, could say about Nature: 'My book is the nature of created things and it is here whenever I need it, to read about God in it.'[22] We can compare the presence of God in the world, to the engine in the aeroplane or the electricity in the cable: without it the aeroplane falls out of the sky. Edith Sitwell tries to express this in a poem called, 'How many Heavens':

> The emeralds are singing in the grasses
> and in the trees, the bells of the long cold are ringing,—
> My blood seems changed to emeralds like the spears of grass
> Beneath the earth piercing and singing.
>
> The flame of the first blade
> Is an angel piercing through the earth to sing
> 'God is everything!
> The grass within the grass, the angel in the angel, flame
> Within the flame, and He is green shade that came
> To be the heart of shade.'
> ...
> He is the sea of ripeness and the sweet apples' emerald lore.
> So you, my flame of grass, my root of the world from which all
> Spring shall grow,
> O you, my hawthorn bough of the stars, now leaning low
> Through the day, for your flowers to kiss my lips, shall know
> He is the core of the heart of love, and He, beyond labouring
> seas, our ultimate shore.

So God is present in all nature. Above all, God is present in persons and in their relationships with one another. By opening up in sacrificial love before the *Thou*, each of us becomes *I*.[23]

---

[22] Quoted by Evagrius of Pontus in *Praktikos* 92, translated in *Evagrius of Pontus: The Greek Ascetic Corpus*, trans. with commentary by Robert Sinkewicz (Oxford University Press, 2003), 112.

[23] See Martin Buber, *I and Thou*, trans. R. G. Smith (T. & T. Clark, 1937).

OUR RELATIONSHIP WITH THE FATHER

Normally, we speak of Christianity as being a relationship with our Lord Jesus, but at the heart of all Jesus's desire for his disciples, was his longing that they should share in his knowledge of the Father. Just as the phrase 'I go to the Father' summarizes Jesus's life, so Jesus's prayer is that all his disciples might receive a new relationship with the Father, and this is effected by the Spirit. At the Last Supper he prays that

> they may all be one. As you, Father, are in me and I am in you, may they also be in us, so that the world may believe that you have sent me. The glory that you have given me I have given them, so that they may be one, as we are one, I in them and you in me, that they may become completely one, so that the world may know that you have sent me and have loved them even as you have loved me. (John 17: 20–3)

Perhaps we can think of 'glory' as 'relationship'? So the Holy Trinity is a mystery in the true sense of that word, a revelation to be adoringly lived in, not rationally analyzed. God in dialogue with himself, a dialogue that is

open, not shut;

inviting, not repelling;

including, not excluding;

giving, not taking.

Here we have God as love as well as being. In this Trinity, humanity has the hope of finding not merely the meaning of unity in the world, but also the meaning of diversity. For all of us find within ourselves a tension between two contradictory drives, the drive for separation and the drive for union. On one hand, we want to be separate from other people, to be distinct, ourselves and not anybody else, working out our own destiny for ourselves. And on the other, we find in ourselves a desire not to be alone but to be united with others, to be open, receptive, a partner. We fulfils ourselves by relating to others, we finds ourselves by losing our autonomous self, in the various involvements of life. As Buber says, 'Through the *Thou*, a man becomes *I*'.[24]

The perfection of God is not to be a monad. But the relationship of the three persons which we glimpse in the earthly ministry of the Lord Jesus hints to us the relationship of the three persons in eternity. This relationship in eternity is the source and origin of the Son's mission in time, continued for us by the Spirit.

The Gospel gives us two pictures of this trinitarian relationship in the Transfiguration and more obviously in the Baptism of the Lord. In the water, Jesus shows us (makes an epiphany) of what it is to be Man, in the dimension of dread. There he takes to himself the whole dimension of Israel's past: he is the new Noah, carrying God's people through the waters of destruction; and thereby

becoming the new Moses,

bringing them out of slavery in Egypt

through the waters of the Red Sea

into the freedom of the promised land.

He is the new Joshua, leading them over Jordan. The descent of the Spirit upon him like a dove recalls the Spirit hovering over the waters of chaos (in the Genesis myth) bringing life and order. But his baptism is not just an identification with the people of Israel in their past; it is an identification with all people in their future. Jesus is no hybrid, with the mind of God in the body of man: he is not half God and half man.

He is altogether one of us, Son of Man,

he is altogether with God, Son of God.

As a human he had to learn as all of us have to learn.

---

[24] Buber, *I and Thou*, 28.

He too was a spiritual traveller;

he was tired, uncertain,

he did not know.

He had to live with the ambiguities and temptations;

he doubted,

he had to struggle with right and wrong, just as we do.

THE HUMANITY OF JESUS

The revelation of God our Saviour is not now going to be in the thunderstorms of Sinai, not even in the still, small voice of silence. The revelation of God is a man among men and women. At Bethlehem and on the Cross and in the waters of Baptism, Jesus enters the tensions and ambiguities of being human. Baptism means identification with the mass of humanity. George Fox used to pray 'that [God] would baptize my heart into a sense of all conditions, that so I might be able to enter into the needs and sorrows of all'.[25] Jesus entered the tensions and ambiguities of being human, including death, for nowhere else do we see the complete solidarity of mankind except in our common death. It is in death that we are all united. So the baptism of Jesus is, above all, an identification with us in our death—a pointing forward to Good Friday. The body in the water, the corpse on the Cross, is the revelation (epiphany) of the goodness of God our Saviour. Jesus comes through the water of death, he enters the Resurrection kingdom and for this reason he is the Lamb of God because he takes away and destroys the sin of the world. For this reason he is Son of God because here, as in eternity, he displays complete filial obedience and love.

Here in the water (that is, in death and on the Cross), we see the epiphany of the three-fold God. The voice of the Father is heard,

---

[25] Quoted in Adoniram Judson Gordon, *In Christ; or, The Believer's Union with his Lord* (Hodder and Stoughton, 1882), 129, n.1.

expressing his wondering delight in his Son. The proof and sign of the Father's delight is his sending of the Spirit. Three distinct persons, not three aspects of one person, not one person with three masks. Augustine describes the Father as love, the Son as the Beloved, and the Spirit as the uniting love.[26] When we human beings know something,

> 'This is my Son, the Beloved, with whom I am well pleased.' (Matt. 3:17)

we go out of ourselves towards the object, which then sends back impressions to us. But in the Holy Trinity, the circle of knowledge and love is *within* God. The Desert Fathers speak of a circular movement of love within the Trinity, a *kyklike kinesis*—a circular movement of love from the Father, through the Spirit, to the Son and back again from the Son, through the Spirit, to the Father.

To love is to know and to be known. Someone gazing at a very accurate picture of themselves might exclaim, 'I am in that picture, and that picture is me.' In a comparable way, Christ is the picture, image and glory of the Father. He is the mirror of the Father's beauty. As Jesus prays in St John's Gospel:

> Father, the hour has come; glorify your Son so that the Son may glorify you. (John 17:1)

> The glory that you have given me I have given them (John 17:22)

In *The Great Divorce,* C. S. Lewis wrote: 'The glory flows into everyone and back again from everyone, like light and mirrors. But the light's the thing.'[27] The person of the Spirit is the love of the Father for his Son and the person of the Spirit is the love of the Son for his Father.

The Divine Life itself flows and exchanges between the three persons. Whatever we know about God, we know that he is total giving of himself. God is himself only by giving himself, by pouring himself out. The Father, the source and origin of Godhead, bestows

---

[26] *De Trinitate* VIII. 10.

[27] C. S. Lewis, *The Great Divorce* (Macmillan, 1946), 82–3.

the fullness of Godhead upon his Son. Nothing of what it means to be God does the Father clutch to himself. Nor does the Son consider equality with the Father something to be tightly clung to, but he too pours himself out, not only towards the Father, but also towards the world. From this *perichoresis* of the three persons there are two further consequences, first the creation of the world.

The creation of the world is not a mere accident; the calling into existence of the world is a necessary consequence, somehow, of this perichoresis between the Persons, God eternally self-giving: the love of God eternally proceeding, within the Godhead. And so somehow God transcends and breaks his boundaries and limits, he creates something other than himself to love. The love of the three persons of the Trinity is a love of wonder and delight in themselves, but in some sense it is not a complete love because it is not creative. Therefore God creates mankind to be the theatre and expression of his love. Mankind however must have a free choice to respond to God with love, and therefore the moment of creation is, for God, the moment of risk, for in some sense he is jeopardizing the future of being God. His commitment to the Cross skews even more starkly how creation involves a self-limitation of God's being God. Nietzsche says, 'God too has his hell: it is his love of man.'[28]

The second consequence of the perichoresis is the gift of the Holy Spirit to mankind at Pentecost. Just as within the Godhead the Spirit proceeds from the Father to the Son, and back to the Father, so in the new creation the Spirit is given by the Father to the new, total Christ, and the Spirit given to us, draws us to the Father. Thus salvation, wholeness, means that we are taken up into the Holy Trinity's own inner love-life.

There are two further consequences of this incredible doctrine of the Trinity. First, our doctrine of humanity. The last chapter of David Jenkins' book, *The Contradiction of Christianity* is called 'The

---

[28] Friedrich Nietzsche, *Thus Spoke Zarathustra*, trans. Clancy Martin (Barnes & Noble Classics, 2005), 79.

Trinity—love in the end'. Somehow it seems to expand to the saying of Nikolas Fedorov, 'The dogma of the Trinity is our social programme.'[29] Jenkins writes:

> The Trinity stands, not for a doctrine but for a way of life which is related to God's life. To reduce 'the Trinity' to doctrine or to metaphysics is to shrink its significance in a deadly way ... Men and women require love. God offers love. ... Thus, what the Trinity symbolizes is the establishment and vindication of an ultimate insight of love ... Human beings have infinite possibilities of relationship and enjoyment which are to be eternally established. ... The Doctrine of the Trinity reflects and represents the discovery of the possibilities of being human, through developing experience of love, ... it speaks of a community and a communion, where love fulfils love, so that everyone is fully human because everyone is fully human. ... The Trinity promises that there is a way of my being me, which will come about by my finding my being in you. And this will come about when and as you are you and I am I.[30]

A second consequence of the doctrine of the Trinity is the possibility of prayer. Through Jesus we pray to our Father, in the power of the Spirit. Our words reach the eternal Father through the mouth of his dear Son. Somehow our prayer becomes a part of the communion of the Son and the Father in the power of the Holy Spirit. The whole Christ—*Totus Christus caput et corpus adorans Patrem*[31] (the whole Christ, head and members, adores the Father)—offers the Father a free and open love necessary for his glory.

---

[29] Nikolas Fedorov, *The Philosophy of Action*, trans. Ludmila Koehler (Institute for the Human Sciences, 1979).

[30] David E. Jenkins, *The Contradiction of Christianity* (SCM Press, 1985), 32.

[31] Augustine, *Enarrationes in Psalmos* 30[2].3, Corpus Christianorum Series Latina 38:192: '[Q]uia et hoc dixit, tristem esse animam suam usque ad mortem, et utique nos ipsi omnes cum illo. Nam sine illo, nos nihil; in illo autem, ipse Christus et nos. Quare? Quia totus Christus caput et corpus.'

> Love is open to receive the Father's love and open to love him in return.

Our High Priest, Jesus, raises us up on his heart to the Father, holding us exposed to the love and life that flows out from the Father, so that we too receive the Spirit, the approbation and delight of the Father, so that we too can hear said over each one of us,

This is my Son, the Beloved, with whom I am well pleased.

(Matt. 3:17)

I offer again two quotations for contemplation. The first from Julian of Norwich, who tells us:

> ... we can do no more but behold him, enjoying, with an high, mighty desire to be all oned into him—and enjoy in his loving and delight in his goodness. And then shall we all come into our Lord, our Self clearly knowing, and God fully having; and we shall endlessly be all had in God: him verily seeing and fulsomely feeling ...[32]

The second is from William of Saint Thierry:

> The Holy Spirit is the love of the Father and the Son, their unity, sweetness, good, kiss, embrace, and whatever else they can have in common in that union of supreme truth and truth in unity, the Holy Spirit becomes for man in regard to God (in a manner appropriate to man), what he is to the Son in regard to the Father, or for the Father in regard to the Son, through unity of substance. The Christian soul in its happiness finds itself standing midway in the embrace and kiss of the Father and the Son in a manner which exceeds description and thought: the man of God is found worthy to become not God, but what God is. That is to say, man becomes through grace, what God is by nature.[33]

---

[32] Julian of Norwich, *Revelations of Divine Love*, 148.

[33] William of Saint Thierry, *Une Abbaye du Sixième au Vingtième Siècle*, ed. Jerry Carfantan, Cistercian Studies, 94 (Cistercian Publications, 1987), 251.

> O God, I have nothing, I am nothing, I desire only one thing, and that is the Lord Jesus. And Christ who is our life shall appear and then we also shall appear with him in glory.

V
WORSHIP

Lord, the eyes of all wait upon thee: thou fillest all things living with plenteousness. May the Lord rejoice in all his works. (Ps. 145:15)

GOD IS SOMEHOW not complete without the love and fellowship his creatures give him. We who are made in the image of God, whom God created out of dust—God needs. So humble is his love that God needs our love and suffers for us. Our love of God, the Holy Spirit, which has been shed abroad in our hearts, this very love we long to return to God, and this love is the same love as the love which is between the Father and his Son.

> Bless the Lord, O my soul, and all that is within me, bless his holy name. (Ps. 103:1)

Sometimes people think that only God in his fullness can bless. That it is God's nature to bless his little creature, us. No, God wants us to bless him, to rejoice in him and to adore him. God wants us to share in the joy that he himself experiences as he fulfils all things and leads all things to their climax.

SIGHT

'Most probably', said G. K. Chesterton, 'we are in Eden still. It is only our eyes that have changed.'[34] How do we see things?

Lord, grant that I may see,
that I may become aware of my blindness,
of things and dimensions of things
that I do not at present see.

---

[34] G. K. Chesterton, *The Defendant* (J. M. Dent, 1922), introduction.

Are our hearts too confused to see the things that are here? Do we see things that are not here but which must be seen? Are there some things that are here—beauty, situations of conflict, the presence of God—that we don't see because we don't want to see them? In *The Little Prince* the Fox says, 'It is only with the heart that one can see rightly; what is essential is invisible to the eye.'[35] Two poems by R. S. Thomas about perception come to mind:

> In Wales there are jewels to gather
> But with the eye only.
> A hill lights up suddenly,
> A field trembles with colour and goes out in its turn.
> In one day you an witness the extent of the spectrum,
> And grow rich with looking.[36]

> I have seen the sun break through
> to illuminate a small field
> for a while, and gone my way
> and forgotten it. But that was the pearl
> of great price, the one field that had
> the treasure in it. I realize now
> that I must give all that I have
> to possess it. Life is not a hurrying
> on to a receding future, nor hankering after
> an imagined past. It is the turning
> aside like Moses to the miracle
> of the lit bush, to a brightness
> that seemed as transitory as your youth
> once, but is the eternity that awaits you.[37]

---

[35] Antoine de Saint-Exupéry, *The Little Prince*, trans. Irene Testot-Ferry, Wordsworth Classics (Wordsworth Editions, 1995), 82.

[36] R. S. Thomas, 'The Small Window', © Elodie Thomas, reproduced with kind permission.

[37] R. S. Thomas, 'The Bright Field', © Elodie Thomas, reproduced with kind permission.

Stopping, turning aside, seeing, recognizing the burning bush we are faced with questions. *Is it one bush?*

   Is it a holy person?

      Is it Mary?

         Is it the Church?

           Is it something even bigger than that?

WONDER

By pondering the things that God has made, we begin to give time to external reality, to the wonder of the gifts. And then to the wonder of the Giver:

> To see each stone,
> each leaf,
> each blade of grass,
> each animal,
> each human face,
> for what it really is:
> an ikon of God,
> a unique manifestation of God's lover's art.
> This material object,
> this person with whom I am talking,
> this moment of time,
> each is holy,
> each is unrepeatable.

The beginning of wonder is to discover the extraordinariness of the ordinary: what Chesterton called the startling wetness of water, and steeliness of steel.[38] Discovering the uniqueness of each thing and each person, we then discover how each points beyond itself to its Creator. And as I see that relationship, I begin to bless. Julian of Norwich's hazelnut is a case in point:

---

[38] G. K. Chesterton in a letter to his fiancée, 8 July 1899.

I looked thereupon with eye of my understanding, and thought: 'What may this be?' And it was generally answered thus, 'It is all that is made.' I marvelled how it might last, for methought it might suddenly have fallen to naught for little[ness]. And I was answered in my understanding: 'it lasteth, and ever shall for that God loveth it.' And so all thing hath the Being by the love of God. In this Little Thing, I saw three properties. The first is that God made it: the second is that God loveth it: the third, that God keepeth it.[39]

And as we begin to be sensitive to God's wonder all around us, we also become more sensitive to God's touching and presence within us. And from the hazelnut, Lady Julian goes on: 'But what those words: maker, keeper, and lover, mean, I cannot tell, until I am so fastened to him that there is no separation between us.' And then, this drives her to make her great prayer: 'God, of your goodness, give me yourself.'

Beginning to see Nature in God, I begin also to see my unique relationship with God. I begin to understand our task to be the priest of creation. A priest is one who makes anamnesis and eucharist. Priests make remembrance before God, and as they make remembrance, they bless. Humanity: created to be the priest and guardian of creation, the burning bush, leading the creation to its fulfilment in God. Unfallen humanity receives its vocation to rejoice in all the good things that the Lord has given us. Joy and wonder in the creation which I offer back to God with thankfulness. G. K. Chesterton puts it memorably,

> You say grace before meals. All right. But I say grace before the concert and the opera, and grace before the play and pantomime, and grace before I open a book, and grace before sketching, painting, swimming, fencing, boxing, walking, playing, dancing and grace before I dip the pen in the ink.[40]

---

[39] Julian of Norwich, *Revelations of Divine Love*, 52.

[40] *Collected Works of G. K. Chesterton*, vol. x, (Ignatius Press, 1994), part I, 43.

As we articulate this thanksgiving and wonder of creation to its Creator, we become the creation's priest, reordering the fallen world into its relationship with God. In the words of the Psalmist:

> I will bless the Lord at all times;
> his praise shall continually be in my mouth.
> My soul makes its boast in the Lord;
> let the humble hear and be glad.
> O magnify the Lord with me,
> and let us exalt his name together.   (Ps. 34:1–3)

So even before the 'eucharistic man' came to pass, even before the Eucharist of the Church, humanity had a eucharist and anamnesis to make. Humanity is required constantly to remember the Giver and to make eucharist to the Giver for his gift. And as the eucharist is made, over the world, there is an epiclesis, a descent (a gift) of the Spirit upon the offered creation. So Vaughan can say, 'Prayer is the world in tune.'[41]

In the Genesis myth, the animals are brought nameless by God, the Creator, before man, his creature. And the man is given the task of naming them, of establishing their role and identity on earth. God wants humanity to be his viceroy and deputy on the earth. Our basic original sin is that we turn away from this eucharistic relationship with the Creator.

We turn from God-centredness to self-centredness.

We no longer bless the Giver for his gifts.

We regard creation and other human beings as our own possession
    to be grasped,
        exploited,
            devoured.

We no longer see others as *theopolis*, in their own unique relationship with God but as objects for our own use. Instead of unifying the earth in a great thanksgiving to God, we divide creation, we divide ourselves off from God.

---

[41] Henry Vaughan, 'The Morning-Watch'.

*Entrusted by God with the gift of freedom,
we deny this freedom to other people.*

*Blessed with the ability to reshape the world,
we misuse that responsibility to destroy creation.*

*We make ugliness,
    pollution,
        waste,
            destruction.*

As Gerard Manley Hopkins put it in 'God's Grandeur':

> Generations have trod, have trod, have trod;
> And all is seared with trade; bleared, smeared with toil;
> And wears man's smudge and shares man's smell...

*Think of the conditions in which human hands have worked
and do work.*

Think of the denial of co-creatorship implied in unemployment.

*Think of the exploitation, competition, class struggle, organized
selfishness that goes on in society.*

*Think of what has happened to the wine that was created to bring
gladness to the heart of humanity.*

In this wine we see both our sinfulness, and also our bringing creation to perfection in its eucharistic relationship with the Creator.

DEATH

In his mercy, God does not allow us to go on living indefinitely in a fallen world and with the consequences of our sin. God sets a merciful limit to our chaos and pain, and this limit is the gift of death. For death is not the end of life, but the beginning of its renewal. God acts like the potter: when the vessel on his wheel has become marred and misused, he breaks the clay to pieces, so as to fashion it anew. Death is an ambiguous gift.

> it is both the consequence of the Fall and the sign
> of the new creation;
>
> it is both separation and union;
>
> it is both hopelessness and hope;
>
> it is both an end and a beginning.

And so because he is completely human, Jesus enters death. This is the great insight of Julian of Norwich:

> Then said our good Lord Jesus Christ: 'Art thou well paid that I suffered for thee?' I said: 'Yea, good Lord, gramercy. Yea, good Lord, blessed mayst thou be.' Then said Jesus, our kind Lord: 'If thou art paid, I am paid: it is a joy, a bliss, and endless liking to me that ever suffered I passion for thee; and if I might suffer more, I would suffer more.'[42]

Jesus is not destroyed by the death he entered. The Father's love is seen to be more powerful, more trustworthy than the enemies of humanity. The Son rises from the dead, and by his rising he delivers us from anxiety and terror. Love is shown to be stronger than hatred, the life of God is seen to be stronger than death. There is no more death, because even death (the place of no God) has now been filled with all the fullness of God. Heaven and earth and even death are now filled with God's glory. There is only the explosion of Easter joy and of eucharistic worship. As Cleopas and his companion discovered at Emmaus:

> 'Were not our hearts burning within us while he was talking to us on the road, while he was opening the scriptures to us?' ... and how he had been made known to them in the breaking of the bread.   (Luke 24:32–5)

Billy Bray, the nineteenth-century Cornish evangelist, once came upon somebody who was looking gloomy, and down in the dust. And he said to him 'Why are you sad, the whole hill of

---

[42] Julian of Norwich, *Revelations of Divine Love*, 94.

Calvary is yours?' Speaking of himself he said, 'I can't help praising the Lord, as I go along the street. I lift one foot and it seems to say 'Glory'. And I lift up the other, and it seems to say 'Amen'. And so I keep on like that all the time that I walk. Heaven and earth are full of thy glory!'[43]

> *God surrounds us with his tenderness and love. We give thanks to God for the love of our parents and our godparents; for those who were our pastors when we were children: for those whose prayer and example have helped us and have led us here.*

---

[43] C. J. Whitmore, 'Flames of Fire: Billy Bray, the Cornish Miner', *The Christian Mission Magazine* (May 1874), 78ff.

VI
EUCHARIST

... give us this bread always (John 6:34)

PERHAPS FAR MORE people than we allow have some form of religious experience. An example of what may be a fairly typical form of this experience is recorded in Waldo Williams' poem 'Between Two Fields'. Williams had an experience as a child on his way to school in Narberth in Pembrokeshire, as he was standing in a gap between two fields. For most of his life he reflected on this experience and he expressed his feelings in this poem. It is quite a curious link with antiquity because Narberth was the place where the medieval romances called the 'Mabinogion' begin. It is somehow as if the other world is very close to that sort of person. It begins just the other side of the ferns, or just around the corner, or the next building—you step over the hedge and there you are, in it. He asks:

> So who was it stood
> there in the middle of this shameless glory, who
> stood holding it all? Of every witness witness,
> the memory of every memory, the life
> of every life? who with a quiet word
> calms the red storms of self, till all
> the labours of the whole wide world
> fold up into this silence.
> And on the silent sea-floor of these fields,
> his people stroll. Somewhere between them,
> through them, around them, there is a new voice
> rising and spilling from its hiding place
> to hold them, a new voice, call it the poet's
> as it was for some of us, the little group

who'd been all day mounting assault
against the harvest with our forks, dragging
the roof-thatch over the heavy meadow. So near,
we came so near then to each other, the quiet huntsman
spreading his net around us.[44]

That quotation brings together many of the threads that these meditations try to unravel. The approach of wonder; the specificity of these individuals and places that God gives to us.

> *The all-encompassing love of God:*
>
> *God's pervading all that is,*
>
> *God the enabler and goal of everything.*
>
> *The trees and the clouds, the whole of those two fields are penetrated and enclosed by God.*
>
> *God is so close to them that he can be described as each witnesses' witness,*
> *each memories' memory,*
> *the life of each life*

Compare Augustine's word to God, *tu autem eras interior intimo meo* (you are more inside me than I am inside myself).[45] Yet God is other and transcendent.

> *He comes from outside, as 'the tranquil calmer of the turmoil of self'.*
>
> *He is the goal and unity and peace for which all these things and people long.*
>
> *He contains and recapitulates it all —*
> *then 'the whole world came somehow into God's stillness'*
> *— and in God's stillness we see not simply God, but other people.*

---

[44] Waldo Williams, 'Between Two Fields' ('Mewn Dau Gae'), from *Dail Pren*, trans. in Rowan Williams, *The Other Mountain* (Carcanet, 2014).

[45] *Confessions*, III.6, 11.

All the heavenly Jerusalem: *And on the two fields, all God's people walked together.* For only in God can we meet one another. The closer we are to the heavenly Father, the closer we shall be to our brothers and sisters. And this is no natural phenomenon, for 'among them, through them, there spread all around them, the Holy Spirit rising out of concealment.' Yes, he had been there all the time. But by being remembered, by anamnesis, by being invoked, by epiclesis, the Holy Spirit descends on to the sacrifice which is creation. And the result 'we are made all one: how close we all grew to one another'. So God's age-long purpose is fulfilled: 'the Silent Hunter was drawing his net around us'.

It is an intensely eucharistic vision of the particular being blessed on the descent of the Spirit; of the taking up of matter into the divine. Paradoxically, the author was a Quaker, one without outward sacraments; although, perhaps like the Desert Fathers whom he resembles in so many ways, perhaps it was for the sake of Christ the sacrament that he felt the inadequacy of other sacraments.

PRIESTHOOD

As we have seen, to bless the Giver is the natural priesthood of humanity. To quote the Psalmist once again:

> I will bless the Lord at all times;
> his praise shall continually be in my mouth.   (Ps. 34:1)

In the Jewish Prayerbook, there are blessings for almost every possible occasion of human experience: on the new moon, on seeing lightning, on hearing thunder, before drinking wine, before eating fruit, on smelling an odorous plant or fruit, on seeing beautiful trees, on seeing trees blossoming for the first time in the year ... An atheist philosopher says, 'he who does not remember the past [he who does not make anamnesis] is condemned to repeat its mistakes.'[46]

---

[46] George Santayana, 'Reason in Common Sense', in *The Sense of Beauty* (1896), vol. 1.

> *To remember,*
> *to praise,*
> *to make anamnesis and Eucharist,*
> *is to be set free from the evil of the past.*
> *It is to establish a limit to evil,*
> *to open the door of hope for the future.*

But we forget and turns away from God; we no longer act as the priest bringing things and people into relationship with God, by remembering and blessing. By ceasing to live eucharistically we fall away from God, his centre.

Jesus, the true Eucharist of the Trinity, enters the world and re-establishes in the midst of death and suffering the eucharistic dimension: the blessing of the Name, the gateway into the kingdom. Jesus gathers together a new people, those who worship the Father. The purpose of the Father's saving will is to gather together into one all the scattered children of God, in particular, the poor, the outsider. Joachim Jeremias says,

> the last supper of Jesus with his disciples, must not be isolated, but should rather be seen as one of a long series of daily meals that they had shared together. For the oriental, every table fellowship is a guarantee of peace, trust, and of brotherhood. Table fellowship with Jesus is far more, for Jesus celebrates with sinners and outcasts ... Hence, the passionate objections of the Pharisees ... ('This man receives sinners and eats with them') who held that the pious could have table fellowship only with the righteous. They understood the intention of Jesus, as being to accord to the outcasts worth before God by eating with them, and they objected to this placing of the sinner on to the same level as the righteous. The fact that the risen Lord eats with his disciples who had forsaken him, means that the disciples are re-admitted into their old fellowship and are forgiven ... the Messiah himself serves them at the Messiah's meal.[47]

---

[47] Joachim Jeremias, *The Eucharistic Words of Jesus* (Blackwell, 1955), 136.

God intended that the created universe through our presence and work as the priest of creation, was to be a harmony, a liturgy, naturally leading its prophet, priest and king (humankind), holy and unspotted to total life in God. The disorder in us and in creation caused by sin makes redemption necessary: that is, the insertion into the disordered, dying world of the new life, so that the disordered world can be restored to order, to harmony, to liturgy. This new, life-creating life is Jesus himself.

In Jesus, liturgy (contemplation, worship, the kingdom of God, or whatever you like to call it) was, and is, continual; because the whole of Jesus's activity is penetrated by his divinity. In Jesus there is no separation between the human and the Divine; nor is there any discontinuity or contradiction between Jesus's life on earth and his being at the same time in the bosom of the Father. For in every action, in every situation, in every encounter, Jesus contemplated the Father. He saw the Father, and in the Father he saw the creation as it is and as it will become. There is, in Jesus no separation between adoring the Father and other activities, between liturgy and non-liturgy, for in every incident and encounter these words of Jesus are true: 'I go to the Father'.

Pre-eminently this going to the Father takes place in the paschal mystery of the Last Supper, Crucifixion, Resurrection, and Ascension. But these earthly events merely reveal in the human situation, and under intense pressure of extreme pain and temptation, what is the whole direction and purpose of the Son's life: to go to the Father. He is our sacrament and the sacraments he shares with us are the means by which the exalted Lord reaches out to us, takes control of us; they are dynamic means by which we are changed into his attitudes, by which we share his life and worship. But we have to learn, that is our *ascesis*, to bless God at all times. We cannot do it naturally as Jesus can. The sacraments are the source and signs of the new creation, of our being taken by Jesus in the power of the Spirit, into the love of the Father. They are the vitalizing acts of the Spirit, bringing life, power, healing where there is only death, separation, sinfulness.

They are the means by which the exalted Saviour conveys his unimaginable power and salvation to his people. Through them he makes all things new. 'He who was on earth in the flesh now continues his work in the sacraments'.[48]

EUCHARIST

All the sacraments are entries—Passovers—into glory. In Baptism and Confirmation we receive the spirit of Glory; we die and are conformed to the image of the Son of God. Our Baptism displays for us the mystery of our predestination, justification and glorification. So that when we are tempted we can cry out with Luther: 'I have been baptized, I am dead and buried in Christ, and I now have his life and resurrection. I live by faith in the Son of God who loved me and gave himself for me.'[49] In Baptism, God sets his love upon us and makes us lovely. The Holy Spirit of Glory: he who is the bond of glory between the Father and the Son, is there given to us in that sacrament.

When we fall short of the glory of God by sin—when we love other people on our own terms, not with God's love—we are restored by the sacrament of Confession. The sacrament of Ordination gives the pastor a share in 'the ministry of glory'. Holy Marriage is the sign and inauguration of the union of all in Christ, when our Lord will be all in all. And when our bodies are sick and tired, they are restored by the prayers and anointing of the Church. He who was on earth in the flesh continues his work in the sacraments.

But above all it is in the holy Eucharist that we can see what God is making of us. Here we do and are what we were created to do and become: full of thanksgiving, rejoicing in the holy attachment of God. For the movement of the Eucharist, just as of the whole of the incarnation, is not simply a descent of the Lord to us; primarily it is our ascent to the Father, a lifting up of restored new manhood to eternal life in God, in our great High Priest, Jesus Christ.

---

[48] St Leo the Great.

[49] Cf. Gal. 2:20.

Who am I when I stand in the Eucharist? First of all, I am a microcosm of the universe, a representative of the world. Freud says something to the effect that every person recapitulates in themselves the history of the human race.[50] So that is what I bring as I stand in the Eucharist.

> I carry people on my heart,
> people who live in us and of us,
> and we bring them as part of our offering,
> as part of our flesh, to God.

But not only in the Eucharist do we direct and bring to the Father the longings and worship of his creation. When the Father looks upon us, he sees in us what his creation is to become; the universe, which at present groans in travail, awaits the glorious freedom of the sons of God. In the Eucharist, we are the first-fruits of his creation, restored to our Adamic dignity, as prophet, priest and king of the world, joining the creation to the kingdom of God in a vast hymn of praise: 'evermore praising thee and saying Holy'. In the Eucharist we become what we are intended to be, as Augustine puts it: 'an Alleluia, from head to foot. We become changed into him of whom we live.'

An Anglo-Saxon manuscript describes the church sanctuary, the place of the altar-table, as the bridal-chamber of the Lamb. The Father has united all things in Christ, things in heaven and things on earth. By Baptism he has already raised us up with Christ and made us sit with him in the heavenly places. If we could see the creation as the Father sees it, as the saints and angels see it, we should see a vast cosmic liturgy. And at the heart of this liturgy is the Trinity's own relationship with itself, its own giving worth and worship to the other members of that divine family, its own inner loveliness, into which we are caught up. The whole creation is being transformed into the loveliness of God. As the Psalmist sang,

> In your light we see light. (Ps. 36:9)

---

[50] Sigmund Freud, *Introductory Lectures on Psycho-Analysis*, standard edn, vol. 15, ed. J. Strachey (Hogarth Press, 1916–17), 199.

Bishop Westcott says: 'Transfiguration is the measure of the capacity of being human. It is the revelation of the potential spirituality of the earthly life in its highest outward form.'[51] The Transfiguration shows us the human body, and indeed, the world, as God intends it to become. There is a hymn from the early church which puts it like this:

> Soon, thou man, shalt dance a dance with God.
> Let us be glad and rejoice and give honour to him.
> The marriage of the Lamb has come.
> Come hither and I will show you the Bride, the Lamb's wife.[52]

Who is the bride? It is the Church, the first-fruits of the creation, the holy church, which in the Eucharist becomes what the creation is destined to become. In the Eucharist, our Lord stoops to us, to assume us to himself; to help us to share in his beauty and dignity. So in the Eucharistic mystery, by an objective act, not by our imagination or wishes, he takes us truly with him into the divine place, into the bosom of the Father, behind the veil. And there we find the whole church of God: the departed, the saints, and we too, though we are still in exile. Standing before the holy Father in the power and new life of the Spirit, with all our freedom and love restored, with our sense of wonder renewed, there is nothing else for us to do but give thanks, to make Eucharist. This 'eucharistizing' is the state of heavenly personhood.

This Eucharist is the worship of all creation; it is the secret meaning and yearning of all creation. Heaven and earth are full in the Eucharist, of God's glory. And this glory is being expressed and articulated by the Church. We have ascended into heaven with Christ and there in the real heavenly glory of the Church, the angels and archangels, and the hosts of heaven, we finally express ourselves to God and we achieve ourselves crying out and shouting 'Holy'. 'By whom, and with whom, and in whom, in the unity of the Holy

---

[51] B. F. Westcott, *The Historic Faith: Short Lectures on the Apostles' Creed* (Wipf and Stock, 2004), 264.

[52] Cf. Rev. 19:7.

Spirit, all honour and glory be unto thee, Father Almighty'. At those words, the restored and new creation, the bread and the wine, are lifted up. Because as, in the radiant majesty of the holy glory, as we in our High Priest stand before the Father in the power of the Spirit, we are led to the very heart of thanksgiving. We remember before the Father what we are most grateful for, the one act of love worthy of the Giver: his own Son's obedience on the Cross. That is what we give thanks for.

> Look, Father, look on his anointed face, and only look on us as found in him.[53]

> *In what he achieved, the whole of our life,*
> *the whole of the world,*
> *finds its fulfilment and achievement.*
> *We are ascended with him.*
> *We share his life in the kingdom.*
> *The Lamb's marriage is here,*
> *and in this glorious and triumphant life,*
> *we share the Lamb's own life.*
> *'Take, eat, this is my body'.*

'What care I about Heaven', cries St John Chrysostom, 'when I myself am become a heaven?'[54] The Kingdom of God, the joy and peace is here. We are transformed in the Holy Spirit into the self-surrender of the Son to his Father and we are transfigured on receiving the Father's love, his only Son, and hearing the voice from heaven.

> This is my Son, the Beloved. (Matt. 17:5)

Reflect, too, on a quote for contemplation from the French-born pioneer of interfaith dialogue, Abhishiktānanda:

---

[53] William Bright, 'And now, O Father, mindful of the Love', in *Ancient & Modern: Hymns for Refreshing Worship* (Canterbury Press, 2013), no. 423.

[54] *St Chrysostom: Homilies on the Gospel of St John and the Epistle to the Hebrews*, Select Library of the Nicene and Post-Nicene Fathers of the Christian Church 14 (Scribner, 1906), 445.

The sacrifice was consummated on the banks of the Ganges at the very source, the eschatological offering had been celebrated. In the sacrifice of the Lamb, everything had finally been brought to completion: every prayer and chant that had been played or sung in these places, everything that had been offered symbolically in the temple or near the flowing river, all the trials and difficulties of the pilgrims, all silence and self-denial of the hermits, everything had finally been gathered up.[55]

And a gentler and less intense statement from the poem by Euros Bowen, 'The Reredos', describing the priest celebrating the Eucharist in a church where there is only plain glass in the east window.

> Not symbols,
> ecclesiastical decor,
> but a clear pane of glass,
> that was the reredos,
> and there was the risk
> of drawing the celebrating's focus
> away
> from the properties of the communion table,
>
> because there,
> in the transparence,
> the greenery of earth was
> flourishing in the sight of morning,
> the river's spate blossoming,
> the air a flight of joy,
> and the sunshine setting
> the clouds on fire,
>
> and I observed
> the eyes of the priest
> as if unawares

---

[55] Abhishiktānanda, *Guru and Disciple*, trans. Heather Sandeman (SPCK, 1974), 174.

placing his hand
upon these gifts
as though
they
were the bread and wine.⁵⁶

The Eucharist draws towards God, includes within the Trinity. But can we say more? Can we dare, in some very anthropomorphic way, to say that our little Eucharist somehow affects the Trinity?

You will recall that there may be at least two kinds of love in God: the love of God which is creative and redemptive, directed outwards towards the world, and the love of God within the Trinity, 'which is a love of delight'.⁵⁷ Perhaps all the fumbling language of theologians about the sacrifice of the mass is an attempt to hint at the ways in which our Eucharist, as re-creating love, may affect the Holy Trinity. Can we, in any sense, dare to say that our Eucharist affords the Trinity a love of delight?

One of the poets has a line that I shall adapt which does, perhaps, hint at this: *The Father kisses his Son in the white bread.*

> By Jesus let us offer the sacrifice of praise continually to God.

---

⁵⁶ Trans. Joseph Clancy.

⁵⁷ Stephen Charnock, *The Complete Works of Stephen Charnock, B.D.*, vol. 3, Nichol's Series of Standard Divines: Puritan period (James Nichol, 1865), 344.

SLG PRESS PUBLICATIONS

FP1	*Prayer and the Life of Reconciliation*	Gilbert Shaw (1969)
FP2	*Aloneness not Loneliness*	Mother Mary Clare SLG (1969)
FP4	*Intercession*	Mother Mary Clare SLG (1969)
FP8	*Prayer: Extracts from the Teaching of Father Gilbert Shaw*	Gilbert Shaw (1973)
FP12	*Learning to Pray*	Mother Mary Clare SLG (1970, rev. 3/2025)
FP15	*Death, the Gateway to Life*	Gilbert Shaw (1971, 3/2024)
FP16	*The Victory of the Cross*	Dumitru Stăniloae (1970, 3/2023)
FP26	*The Message of Saint Seraphim*	Irina Gorainov (1974)
FP28	*Julian of Norwich: Four Studies to Commemorate the Sixth Centenary of the Revelations of Divine Love*	Sister Benedicta Ward SLG, Sister Eileen Mary SLG, Sister Mary Paul SLG, A. M. Allchin (1973, 3/2022)
FP43	*The Power of the Name: The Jesus Prayer in Orthodox Spirituality*	Kallistos Ware (1974)
FP46	*Prayer and Contemplation* and *Distractions are for Healing*	Robert Llewelyn (1975, rev. 4/2025)
FP48	*The Wisdom of the Desert Fathers*	trans. Sister Benedicta Ward SLG (1975)
FP50	*Letters of Saint Antony the Great*	trans. Derwas Chitty (1975, 2/2021)
FP54	*From Loneliness to Solitude*	Roland Walls (1976)
FP55	*Theology and Spirituality*	Andrew Louth (1976, rev. 1978, 3/2024)
FP61	*Kabir: The Way of Love and Paradox*	Sister Rosemary SLG (1977)
FP62	*Anselm of Canterbury: A Monastic Scholar*	Sister Benedicta Ward SLG (1973, 2/2024)
FP67	*Mary and the Mystery of the Incarnation: An Essay on the Mother of God in the Theology of Karl Barth*	Andrew Louth (1977, 2/2024)
FP68	*Trinity and Incarnation in Anglican Tradition*	A. M. Allchin (1977, rev. 2/2025)
FP70	*Facing Depression*	Gonville ffrench-Beytagh (1978, 2/2020)
FP71	*The Single Person*	Philip Welsh (1979)
FP72	*The Letters of Ammonas, Successor of St Antony*	trans. Derwas Chitty, introd. Sebastian Brock (1979, 2/2023)
FP74	*George Herbert, Priest and Poet*	Kenneth Mason (1980)
FP75	*A Study of Wisdom: Three Tracts by the Author of The Cloud of Unknowing*	trans. Clifton Wolters (1980)
FP81	*The Psalms: Prayer Book of the Bible*	Dietrich Bonhoeffer, trans. Sister Isabel SLG (1982, rev. 3/2025)
FP82	*Prayer & Holiness: The Icon of Man Renewed in God*	Dumitru Stăniloae (1982, rev. 2/2023)
FP85	*Walter Hilton: Eight Chapters on Perfection & Angels' Song*	trans. Rosemary Dorward (1983, rev. 3/2024)
FP88	*Creative Suffering*	Iulia de Beausobre (1989)
FP90	*Bringing Forth Christ: Five Feasts of the Child Jesus by St Bonaventure*	trans. Eric Doyle OFM (1984, 3/2024)
FP92	*Gentleness in John of the Cross*	Thomas Kane (1985, rev. 2/2025)
FP94	*Saint Gregory Nazianzen: Selected Poems*	trans. John McGuckin (1986, 2/2024)
FP95	*The World of the Desert Fathers: Stories and Sayings from the Anonymous Series of the Apophthegmata Patrum*	trans. Columba Stewart OSB (1986, 2/2020)
FP104	*Growing Old with God*	Timothy N. Rudd (1988, 2/2020)
FP106	*Julian Reconsidered*	Kenneth Leech, Sister Benedicta Ward SLG (1988, rev. 2/2024)
FP108	*The Unicorn: Meditations on the Love of God*	Harry Galbraith Miller (1989)

FP109 *The Creativity of Diminishment*　　　　　　　　　　　Sister Anke (1990)
FP110 *Called to be Priests*　　　　　　　Hugh Wybrew (1989, updated 2/2024)
FP111 *A Kind of Watershed: An Anglican Lay View of Sacramental Confession*
　　　　　　　　　　　　　　　　Christine North (1990, updated 2/2022)
FP116 *Jesus, the Living Lord*　　　　　　　　　Bishop Michael Ramsey (1992)
FP120 *The Monastic Letters of Saint Athanasius the Great*
　　　　　　　　　　　　trans. and introd. Leslie Barnard (1994, 2/2023)
FP122 *The Hidden Joy*　　　　　　　Sister Jane SLG, ed. Dorothy Sutherland (1994)
FP124 *Prayer of the Heart: An Approach to Silent Prayer and Prayer in the Night*
　　　　　　　　　　　　　　　　　　　　　Alexander Ryrie (1995, 3/2020)
FP126 *Evelyn Underhill, Anglican Mystic: Two Centenary Essays*
　　　　　　　　　A. M. Allchin, Bishop Michael Ramsey (1977, rev. 4/2025)
FP127 *Apostolate and the Mirrors of Paradox*
　　　　　　　　　　　Sydney Evans, ed. Andrew Linzey & Brian Horne (1996)
FP128 *The Wisdom of Saint Isaac the Syrian*　　　　　　Sebastian Brock (1997)
FP129 *Saint Thérèse of Lisieux: Her Relevance for Today*　Sister Eileen Mary SLG (1997)
FP130 *Expectations: Five Addresses for Those Beginning Ministry*　Sister Edmée SLG (1997, 2/2024)
FP131 *Scenes from Animal Life: Fables for the Enneagram Types*
　　　　　　　　　　　　Waltraud Kirschke, trans. Sister Isabel SLG (1998)
FP132 *Praying the Word of God: The Use of Lectio Divina*　Charles Dumont OCSO (1999)
FP133 *Love Unknown: Meditations on the Death and Resurrection of Jesus*
　　　　　　　　　　　　　　　　　　　　　　John Barton (1999, 2/2024)
FP134 *The Hidden Way of Love: Jean-Pierre de Caussade's Spirituality of Abandonment*
　　　　　　　　　　　　　　　　　　　　Barry Conaway (1999, rev. 2/2025)
FP135 *Shepherd and Servant: The Spiritual Theology of Saint Dunstan*　Douglas Dales (2000)
FP137 *Pilgrimage of the Heart*　　　　　　　Sister Benedicta Ward SLG (2001)
FP138 *Mixed Life*　　Walter Hilton, trans. Rosemary Dorward (2001, enlarged rev. 3/2024)
FP139 *In the Footsteps of the Lord: The Teaching of Abba Isaiah of Scetis*
　　　　　　　　　　　　John Chryssavgis, Luke Penkett (2001, 2/2023)
FP140 *A Great Joy: Reflections on the Meaning of Christmas*　Kenneth Mason (2001)
FP141 *Bede and the Psalter*　　　　　　Sister Benedicta Ward SLG (2002, 2/2024)
FP142 *Abhishiktananda: A Memoir of Dom Henri Le Saux*　Murray Rogers, David Barton (2003)
FP143 *Friendship in God: The Encounter of Evelyn Underhill & Sorella Maria of Campello*
　　　　　　　　　　　　　　　　　　　　A. M. Allchin (2003, rev. 2/2025)
FP144 *Christian Imagination in Poetry and Polity: Some Anglican Voices from Temple to Herbert*
　　　　　　　　　　　　　　　　　　　　　Bishop Rowan Williams (2004)
FP145 *The Reflections of Abba Zosimas: Monk of the Palestinian Desert*
　　　　　　　　　　　trans. and introd. John Chryssavgis (2005, 3/2022)
FP146 *The Gift of Theology: The Trinitarian Vision of Ann Griffiths and Elizabeth of Dijon*
　　　　　　　　　　　　　　　　　　　　　　　　A. M. Allchin (2005)
FP147 *Sacrifice and Spirit*　　　　　　　　　Bishop Michael Ramsey (2005)
FP148 *Saint John Cassian on Prayer*　　　　trans. A. M. Casiday (2006, 2/2024)
FP149 *Hymns of Saint Ephrem the Syrian*　　trans. Mary Hansbury (2006, 2/2024)
FP150 *Suffering: Why All this Suffering? What Do I Do about It?*
　　　　　　　　Reinhard Körner OCD, trans. Sister Avis Mary SLG (2006)
FP151 *A True Easter: The Synod of Whitby 664 AD*　Sister Benedicta Ward SLG (2007, 2/2023)
FP152 *Prayer as Self-Offering*　　　　　　　　　　Alexander Ryrie (2007)
FP153 *From Perfection to the Elixir: How George Herbert Fashioned a Famous Poem*
　　　　　　　　　　　　　　　　　　　Benedick de la Mare (2008, 2/2024)
FP154 *The Jesus Prayer: Gospel Soundings*　　Sister Pauline Margaret CHN (2008)

FP 155   *Loving God Whatever: Through the Year with Sister Jane*   Sister Jane SLG (2006)
FP 156   *Prayer and Meditation for a Sleepless Night*
                                              SISTERS OF THE LOVE OF GOD (1993, 3/2024)
FP 157   *Being There: Caring for the Bereaved*   John Porter (2009)
FP 158   *Learn to Be at Peace: The Practice of Stillness*   Andrew Norman (2010)
FP 159   *From Holy Week to Easter*   George Pattison (2010)
FP 160   *Strength in Weakness: The Scandal of the Cross*   John W. Rogerson (2010)
FP 161   *Augustine Baker: Frontiers of the Spirit*   Victor de Waal (2010, rev. 2/2025)
FP 162   *Out of the Depths*
                 Gonville ffrench-Beytagh; epilogue Wendy Robinson (1990, 2/2010)
FP 163   *God and Darkness: A Carmelite Perspective*
                                      Gemma Hinricher OCD, trans. Sister Avis Mary SLG (2010)
FP 164   *The Gift of Joy*   Curtis Almquist SSJE (2011)
FP 165   *'I Have Called You Friends': Suggestions for the Spiritual Life Based on
          the Farewell Discourses of Jesus*   Reinhard Körner OCD (2012)
FP 166   *Leisure*   Mother Mary Clare SLG (2012)
FP 167   *Carmelite Ascent: An Introduction to Saint Teresa and Saint John of the Cross*
                                                         Mother Mary Clare SLG (1973, rev. 2/2012)
FP 168   *Ann Griffiths and Her Writings*   Llewellyn Cumings (2012)
FP 169   *The Our Father*   Sister Benedicta Ward SLG (2012)
FP 171   *The Spiritual Wisdom of the Syriac Book of Steps*   Robert A. Kitchen (2013)
FP 172   *The Prayer of Silence*   Alexander Ryrie (2012)
FP 173   *On Tour in Byzantium: Excerpts from The Spiritual Meadow of John Moschus*
                                                                   Ralph Martin SSM (2013)
FP 174   *Monastic Life*   Bonnie Thurston (2016)
FP 175   *Shall All Be Well? Reflections for Holy Week*   Graham Ward (2015)
FP 176   *Solitude and Communion: Papers on the Hermit Life*   ed. A. M. Allchin (2015)
FP 177   *The Prayers of Jacob of Serugh*   ed. Mary Hansbury (2015)
FP 178   *The Monastic Hours of Prayer*   Sister Benedicta Ward SLG (2016)
FP 179   *The Desert of the Heart: Daily Readings with the Desert Fathers*
                                                   trans. Sister Benedicta Ward SLG (2016)
FP 180   *In Company with Christ: Lent, Palm Sunday, Good Friday & Easter to Pentecost*
                                                                   Sister Benedicta Ward SLG (2016)
FP 181   *Lazarus: Come Out! Reflections on John 11*   Bonnie Thurston (2017)
FP 182   *Unknowing & Astonishment: Meditations on Faith for the Long Haul*
                                                                   Christopher Scott (2018)
FP 183   *Pondering, Praying, Preaching: Romans 8*   Bonnie Thurston (2019, 2/2021)
FP 184   *Shem'on the Graceful: Discourse on the Solitary Life*
                                                   trans. and introd. Mary Hansbury (2020)
FP 185   *God Under My Roof: Celtic Songs and Blessings*   Esther de Waal (2020)
FP 186   *Journeying with the Jesus Prayer*   James F. Wellington (2020)
FP 187   *Poet of the Word: Re-reading Scripture with Ephraem the Syrian* Aelred Partridge OC (2020)
FP 188   *Identity and Ritual*   Alan Griffiths (2021)
FP 189   *River of the Spirit: The Spirituality of Simon Barrington-Ward* Andy Lord (2021)
FP 190   *Prayer and the Struggle against Evil*   John Barton, Daniel Lloyd,
                                                                   James Ramsay, Alexander Ryrie (2021)
FP 191   *Dante's Spiritual Journey: A Reading of the Divine Comedy* Tony Dickinson (2021)
FP 192   *Jesus the Undistorted Image of God*   John Townroe (2022)
FP 193   *Our Deepest Desire: Prayer, Fasting & Almsgiving in the Writings of
          Saint Augustine of Hippo*   Sister Susan SLG (2022)

FP194	Lent with George Herbert	Tony Dickinson (2022)
FP195	Four Ways to the Cross	Tony Dickinson (2022)
FP196	Anselm of Canterbury, Teacher of Prayer	Sister Benedicta Ward SLG (2022)
FP197	With One Heart and Mind: Prayers out of Stillness	Anthony Kemp (2023)
FP198	Sayings of the Urban Fathers & Mothers	James Ashdown (2023)
FP199	Doors	Sister Raphael SLG (2023)
FP200	Monastic Vocation	SISTERS OF THE LOVE OF GOD, Bishop Rowan Williams (2021)
FP201	An Ecology of the Heart: Faith Through the Climate Crisis	Duncan Forbes (2023)
FP202	'In the image of the Image': Gregory of Nyssa's Opposition to Slavery	Adam Couchman (2023)
FP203	Gregory of Nyssa and the Sins of Asia Minor	Jonathan Farrugia (2023)
FP204	Discovery	Arthur Bell (2023)
FP205	Living Healing: The Spirituality of Leanne Payne	Andy Lord (2023)
FP206	Still Listening: Sowing the Seeds of the Jesus Prayer	Bruce Batstone CJN (2023)
FP207	Julian of Norwich: Four Essays to Commemorate 650 Years of the Revelations of Divine Love	Bishop Graham Usher, Father Colin CSWG, Sister Elizabeth Ruth Obbard OC, Mother Hilary Crupi OJN (2023)
FP208	TIME	Dumitru Stăniloae, Kallistos Ware (2023)
FP209	Pearls of Life: A Lifebelt for the Spirit	Tony Dickinson (2024)
FP210	The Way and the Truth and the Life: An Exploration by a Follower of the Way	James Ramsay (2024)
FP211	Cosmos, Crisis & Christ: Essays of Wendy Robinson	Wendy Robinson (2024)
FP212	Towards a Theology of Psychotherapy: The Spirituality of Wendy Robinson	Andrew Louth (2024)
FP213	Immersed in God and the World: Living Priestly Ministry	Andy Lord (2024)
FP214	The Road to Emmaus: A Sculptor's Journey through Time	Rodney Munday (2024)
FP215	Prayer Too Deep for Words	Sister Edmée SLG (2024)
FP216	The Prayers of St Isaac of Nineveh	Sebastian Brock (2024)
FP217	Two Medieval English Saints: Cuthbert and Alban	Sister Benedicta Ward SLG (2024)
FP218	Encountering the Depths	Mother Mary Clare SLG (1981, rev. 3/2024)
FP219	Conflict and Concord	Sister Susan SLG, Bishop Humphrey Southern, Bronwen Neil, Sister Rosemary SLG, Sister Clare-Louise SLG (2024)
FP220	Divine Love in the Song of Songs	Sister Edmée SLG (2024)
FP221	Zeal for the Faith: An Introduction to Christian-Muslim Dialogue	Tony Dickinson (2024)
FP222	Bernard & Abelard	Sister Edmée SLG (2024)
FP223	Eliot's Transitions: T. S. Eliot's Search for Identity and the Society of the Sacred Mission at Kelham Hall	Vincent Strudwick (2024)
FP224	Landscape, Soul and Spirit: Ecology, Prayer and Robert Macfarlane	Andy Lord (2025)
FP225	Our Home is in God	John Townroe (2025)
FP226	Signs of the Times: A Brief Survey of the Bible's Apocalyptic Writings	Tony Dickinson (2025)
FP227	And We Shall be Changed: Christian Reflections on Death and Dying	James Ramsay (2025)
FP228	Journeys into the Bible	Sister Edmée SLG (2025)
FP229	Directions	Sister Edmée SLG (2025)
FP230	Loving Yourself	Richard Frost (2025)
FP231	Angels	Sister Raphael SLG (2025)
FP232	Contemplative Church: Pondering Church in Challenging Times	Andy Lord (2025)
FP233	Stations of the Cross	Donald McChesney, Jean-Bernard Lalanne (2025)
FP234	Being Christian among Britain's Muslims	Nicholas Heale (2025)
FP235	Create in me a Clean Heart	James Coutts (2025)

CONTEMPLATIVE POETRY SERIES

CP1	*Amado Nervo: Poems of Faith and Doubt*	trans. John Gallas (2021)
CP2	*Anglo-Saxon Poets: The High Roof of Heaven*	trans. John Gallas (2021)
CP3	*Middle English Poets: Where Grace Grows Ever Green*	ed. John Gallas (2021)
CP4	*The Voice inside Our Home: Selected Poems*	Edward Clarke (2022)
CP5	*Women & God: Drops in the Sea of Time*	trans. and ed. John Gallas (2022)
CP6	*Gabrielle de Coignard & Vittoria Colonna: Fly Not Too High*	trans. John Gallas (2022)
CP7	*Chancing on Sanctity: Selected Poems*	James Ramsay (2022)
CP8	*Gabriela Mistral: This Far Place*	trans. John Gallas (2023)
CP9	*Henry Vaughan & George Herbert: Divine Themes and Celestial Praise*	ed. Edward Clarke (2023)
CP10	*Love Will Come with Fire: Anthology*	SISTERS OF THE LOVE OF GOD (2023)
CP11	*Touchpapers: Anthology*	coll. and trans. John Gallas (2023)
CP12	*Seasons of my Soul: Selected Poems*	Clare McKerron (2023)
CP13	*Reinhard Sorge: Take Flight to God*	trans. John Gallas (2024)
CP14	*Embertide: Encountering Saint Frideswide*	Romola Parish (2024)
CP15	*Thomas Campion: Made All of Light*	ed. and introd. Julia Craig-McFeely (2024)
CP16	*When God Hides: Selected Poems*	Joseph Evans (2025)

VESTRY GUIDES

VG1	*The Visiting Minister: How to Welcome Visiting Clergy to Your Church*	Paul Monk (2021)
VG2	*Help! No Minister! or Please Take the Service*	Paul Monk (2022)
VG3	*The Liturgy of the Eucharist: An Introductory Guide*	Paul Monk (2024)

www.slgpress.co.uk

The Sisters of the Love of God is an Anglican community of women religious living a contemplative monastic life.

To learn more about the Community and the Convent of the Incarnation at Fairacres, Oxford, see our website www.slg.org.uk.

As well as supporting those seeking to follow a vocation to the monastic life, the Community has a number of forms of association for those who feel drawn to share in the Sisters' life of prayer: Fellowship of the Love of God, Companions, Priests Associate or Oblate Sisters.

For more information email sisters@slg.org.uk or write to The Reverend Mother, Convent of the Incarnation, Parker Street, Oxford, OX4 1TB, UK.